Leading Change While Loving People

T0304219

Filled with stories of successful social change leadership in diverse contexts, this book demonstrates that the best change agents love the people involved most of all.

Many people have experienced change trauma under leaders whose agenda was more important than anything—or anyone—else, so it is no wonder that change failure rates are often reported as 40% to 70%. There is another way: change leaders who work to solve some of the world's toughest problems realize that working with others is necessary to accomplishing a social change mission. This book shares the insights of those who lead social change in the non-profit sector, and shows how they catalyze the urgency for, connect people toward, and continue momentum for a desired change. Their stories reveal three interconnected dimensions of leading change: people (relationships for change), process (communicating for change), and purpose (the change mission). Ultimately, readers will learn that strengthening social capital (people), centering marginal voices (process), and aligning stakeholders to the change mission (purpose) are critical to the work of change agents who value relationships.

Leveraging well-known models and elevating little-heard voices, this book flips the script of conventional leadership books by focusing on non-profit social change leaders rather than business titans. Students, managers, and leaders across sectors will value these new insights, along with a relationally focused process and strategy for leading change and practical tips and recommendations for implementation.

Yulee Lee holds a BA in Political Science from Tufts University, a MA in Public Policy from the University of Chicago, and a PhD in Educational Studies with a concentration in Organizational Leadership from Trinity International University. She has served in the non-profit sector for over 20 years in the areas of re-vitalization, innovation, culture change, and diversity, equity, and inclusion. In addition, she's worked in government on the local and national levels, and directed strategy for service learning in higher education while also teaching at the graduate level on the topics of organizational and change leadership. Yulee also speaks, coaches, and consults organizations on change strategy through her non-profit The Change Leadership Institute. Ultimately, Yulee is passionate about collaborating for change in systems to reflect greater human dignity and flourishing for the vulnerable.

Leading Change While Loving People

Change Management Insights from the Non-profit Sector

Yulee Lee

Routledge
Taylor & Francis Group

NEW YORK AND LONDON

Cover image: ExpressIPhoto/Getty Images

First published 2023
by Routledge
605 Third Avenue, New York, NY 10158

and by Routledge
4 Park Square, Milton Park, Abingdon, Oxon, OX14 4RN

Routledge is an imprint of the Taylor & Francis Group, an informa business

Library of Congress Cataloguing-in-Publication Data
Names: Lee, Yulee, author.
Title: Leading change while loving people : change management insights
from the non-profit sector / Yulee Lee.
Description: New York, NY : Routledge, 2023. | Includes bibliographical
references and index.
Identifiers: LCCN 2022029267 | ISBN 9781032223520 (hardback) |
ISBN 9781032223490 (paperback) | ISBN 9781003272243 (ebook)
Subjects: LCSH: Organizational change--Management. | Leadership. |
Nonprofit organizations--Management.
Classification: LCC HD58.8 .L4237 2023 | DDC 658.4/06--dc23/eng/
20220714
LC record available at https://lccn.loc.gov/2022029267

ISBN: 978-1-032-22352-0 (hbk)
ISBN: 978-1-032-22349-0 (pbk)
ISBN: 978-1-003-27224-3 (ebk)

DOI: 10.4324/9781003272243

Typeset in Sabon
by MPS Limited, Dehradun

To Dave and Dylan – my two most favorite humans in the world.

Contents

Introduction: Change the Way You Lead Change

"I love change!" I know many leaders who would make that same statement until they lead a change process. It is at this point when the idealistic visions of change are tempered by the realities of volatility, uncertainty, complexity, and ambiguity, or VUCA[1] for short. Together, these four words aptly describe the world in which we live, and most of us (I hope!) have come to terms with the uncontrollable and ever-changing environment that surrounds us. However, what can be more difficult for us to embrace is how these combined four words can describe the people we seek to partner with in leading change. That's because we don't treat people as partners, or as co-creators, in the change process. Rather, we take the easier approach, which is to lead change through command, control, and fear tactics. This book calls us to change the way we lead change: A people-centric way that involves a process characterized by care, collaboration, and life-giving measures that put people first. A process that brings people together, appreciates the power that exists in every human being, and leverages our collective abilities to benefit the world. Ultimately, to love change is meaningless if we don't love people.

How Did I Arrive at This Conviction?

During my early years of leading change, I led mostly by instinct. My instincts told me to always love people more than the change itself because what good is change if people are wounded along the way? As people responded to my leadership with high engagement and enthusiasm, I learned that most people had experienced change trauma under leaders who led change with no regard for anyone other than themselves. In fact, research reveals "organizational change may be construed as a major emotional, even traumatic event, for many people" (Smollan, Sayers, and Matheny 2010, 15). To these "leaders," their change agenda was of utmost priority, and they did anything to achieve it even if people were hurt along the way. I consider leading change in

DOI: 10.4324/9781003272243-1

such a way as a form of malpractice. No wonder the rate of change success is so low. Although the range of failure rates varies, research states that change success hovers around 25–30% (Kotter 1995; Miller 2001; Higgs and Rowland 2005)! Now, as a change leader with more than 15 years' experience leading change in diverse contexts, I am committed to leading change for and with people. I'm excited to share research from non-profit change leaders that illumines a people-centric way to lead change, which I believe is key to change success.

What We Know—Current Research and Practice

Gaps in Research

Although non-profit sector research has expanded significantly over the last decade, "our understanding of the role of these institutions is still limited and data coverage frequently remains patchy" (Anheier 2014). Several gaps in the literature exist due to the sheer diversity of types and services of non-profit organizations in confluence with the complexity of their operations that address some of the world's most difficult problems.

Non-profit social change organizations are a context that is "largely unrepresented in academic leadership[2] or collaborative governance literature" (Ospina and Foldy 2010, 303). Leadership research has primarily focused on the for-profit sector (Kotter 1996; Adair 2002; Bennis and Nanus 2004). The current research about non-profit leaders focuses mostly on board and governance issues within the United States (Hailey and James 2004). Therefore, generally little is known about change agent leaders in the non-profit sector, but especially those who lead non-profit organizations that have a global reach and social change impact outside the United States. There is insufficient literature with research about how non-profit leaders design and execute "planned change processes in cross-cultural settings" (Cummings and Worley 2015, 746). With cross-cultural work becoming more of a reality for organizations around the world, Cummings and Worley note that social change organizations that are internationally networked may provide opportunities for future research to address the gap in literature (2015).

Although non-profit organizations influence change in both individuals and society through a variety of efforts (Drucker 1990), the literature that connects non-profits to their social change role has mainly focused on their political advocacy efforts (Child and Gronbjerg 2007; Schmid et al. 2008; Kimberlin 2010; Mosley and Ros 2011; Mellinger 2014). Almog-Bar and Schmid's literature review (2014) highlights this connection with research that centers non-profit social influence around shaping policy and government decisions without recognizing the additional ways non-profits influence social change. Current literature, however, suggests that non-profits influence social change through their relationships with various stake-holders, especially on the community level, as well as through non-profits' own efforts to internally adapt to societal changes (Shier and Graham 2013; Shier et al. 2014). Further, Thompson argues that "the main world of the social entrepreneur is the voluntary [non-profit] sector" (2002, 413), thereby affirming that the non-profit sector is ripe for further research in social entrepreneurship and innovation (Weerawardena and Mort 2012). Even still, gaps in the literature exist as scholars analyze social change by relying on descriptive case studies of individual organizations or on populations that use non-profit services (Boyd and Wilmoth 2006; Shier and Graham 2013; Spergel and Grossman 1997).

Gaps in Practice

Practically, non-profit leaders self-report that "being able to communicate effectively" is one of their biggest challenges and obstacles to success (Brothers and Sherman 2012, 159), thereby necessitating further research to understand how non-profit change agents develop collaborative social networks of relationships to fulfill their mission in changing environments (Ott and Dicke 2016). Communication has often been linked to leadership as a linear form of influence through message transmission (Ruben and Gigliotti 2016). However, practitioners need to rethink understanding of leadership through the lens of communication that reframes leadership as a process of social influence where people relate to one another and their environment (Ruben and Stewart 2016).

In addition, non-profit organizations need greater capacity for learning and building relationships in order to quickly respond to complex social problems in our constantly changing world (Hinrichs and Richardson 2015). Although research on organizational learning is available, a gap in research on organizational learning in non-profit settings continues to exist (Perkins et al. 2007). Attempted research focuses on small, local non-profit service organizations that do not provide adequate research for transfer (Florin et al. 1992) within larger non-profit organizations. With the lack of contextually relevant research, larger non-profit organizations struggle to transfer and execute known for-profit practices into their systems, "a large proportion of organizations are not aware of these practices," and "still others resist applying them" (Colvin 2000; Cummings and Worley 2015). Several scholars note that "future research must establish effective intervention methods to help nonprofits create new structures, processes, and cultures for the learning, development, and empowerment of members and clients, or the organization as a whole, and of the community it serves" (Perkins et al. 2007, 325).

Further, the increase in external challenges faced by non-profit organizations has caught the attention of researchers, who argue that non-profits should adopt more entrepreneurial postures in their work (Weerawardena, McDonald, and Mort 2010; Weerawardena and Sullivan Mort 2012) and pursue practices that are more innovative (Weerawardena, McDonald, and Mort 2010; Jaskyte 2004; McDonald 2007). However, little research exists on how non-profit organizations work toward sustainability in the face of challenging external influences, or how sustainability issues thereby influence non-profit strategy (Weerawardena, McDonald, and Mort 2010).

What We Need—New Research and Practice

Based on the above research and practice gaps, a study of non-profit change agent leaders who influence social change necessitates an understanding of how they facilitate a purposeful interaction between thinking, talking, and learning about change that drives collective action in collaboration with people both internal and external to the organization.

The purpose of this book is to provide new research that explores the relational communication strategies of change agents in non-profit organizations.

Specifically, the following research questions guided my study:

1   In relationship with others, how do non-profit change agents catalyze a sense of urgency for a desired change?
2   In relationship with others, how do non-profit change agents connect people toward a desired change?
3   In relationship with others, how do non-profit change agents continue momentum for a desired change?

Through research, I'll unlock insights from change leaders in the non-profit sector who influence social change,[3] which is change that is distinguished by the following attributes: (1) it is aimed at creating innovative change on behalf of others; (2) it addresses the root causes of social problems; (3) it is collaborative; (4) it requires new learning; and (5) it is not simple (Komives, Wagner, and Associates 2017). In addition, this research conceptualizes social change in the context of communicative processes that happen in relationships as a way to develop collective impact directed at disrupting and transforming dominant, exclusive, and/or violent social systems (adapted from Dutta 2011). Social change can take place both inside and outside the organization, especially when learning is required as part of the change process.

Traditional change models operate under the assumption that we live in a world that is stable, predictable, and controllable (Burnes 2004; Uhl-Bien, Marion, and McKelvey 2007; Stroh 2015). Traditional approaches to change are helpful in addressing linear problems with available solutions that create stability within an organization (Komives, Wagner, and Associates 2017). However, leading social change is "organic" and requires new ways of thinking (Stroh 2015; Komives, Wagner, and Associates 2017). Organic change "occurs in systems not compartments, is ongoing not episodic, is exponential not linear, and can be influenced but not controlled" (Komives, Wagner, and Associates 2017, 205). Rapid social change creates tension within organizations as they are challenged not only to constantly adapt and learn new ways of being and working with one another internally, but to also engage our world as socially responsible citizens. Increasingly, corporate organizations participate as socially responsible citizens in order to contribute to social change and a better world, but non-profit organizations can be an example of how to operate with a social change mission through social influence (Mirvis 2017).

The rapid and interdependent nature of change necessitates a leader who is able to navigate complexity while simultaneously sustaining him- or herself, others, and the organization throughout the transitions of change processes that can include an ebb and flow between different kinds and models of change (planned, directed, or iterative changing) at different points in time (Buono and Kerber 2010; Higgs and Rowland 2010; Van de Ven and Sun 2011; Kerber and Buono 2018; Colwill 2021). Increasingly, the skill sets of change agent leaders include the ability to discern future trends and needs, diagnose present-day challenges, lead and act on change agendas, collaborate with a diverse base of stakeholders, and remain courageous (Baer, Duin, and Bushway 2015; Colwill 2021).

The non-profit change leaders in my study work to solve some of the world's toughest problems. Their shared perspective is that working with others is necessary to accomplishing a social change mission. We can learn from those who lead social change in the non-profit sector as they share stories about how they catalyze the urgency for, connect people toward, and continue momentum for a desired change. Their stories reveal three interconnected dimensions of leading change: people (relationships for change), process (communicating for change), and purpose (the change mission). Ultimately, my research reveals that strengthening social capital (people), centering marginal voices (process), and aligning stakeholders to the change mission (purpose) are critical to the work of change agents who value relationships. These change leaders defied the research on change failure through their unique ability to lead social change through relationships and strategic communication.

Specifically, non-profit change agents valued the process of change-making just as much as, or even more than, the change itself. Their propensity toward relational connection influenced the strategies they chose to move change forward. Further, the non-profit change agents in my research possessed a combination of humility, an awareness of change complexity, and deep respect for every human being—all of which interacted in the change process to prioritize communication that strengthened partnerships and collaboration with others. Recognition of the power of collective social change also gave non-profit change agents the unique role of reweaving the frayed social fabric of our world.

As such, the non-profit sector and its leaders can provide insight into how social change and innovation can take place through relational influence, which involves the need to focus change around communicative strategies and practices (Van Loon 2017). Understanding how the connection between communication and relationships influences a social change process would provide clarifying insight into the complexity of non-profit leadership, as well as reveal how the non-profit sector can continue to learn and share generative practices across institutions that bridge future collaborative efforts.

Research Sample

My research sample comprises 26 change agents of non-profit organizations. I used as many personal connections as possible to pursue initial contact with leaders who were known to have had at least two to five years of oversight influence over the organization's social change mission as well as consistent engagement with stakeholders both inside and outside the organization. Two to five years of experience were chosen to include participants who have experienced a journey of change with their organization. I aimed for a purposeful sample (Patton 2015) in order to "discover, understand, and gain insight" (Merriam and Tisdell 2016, 96) from non-profit change agent leaders, thereby securing a "sample from which the most can be learned" (Merriam and Tisdell 2016, 96). Purposeful sampling allows in-depth exploration of "information-rich cases" (Patton 2015, 53, emphasis in original). Information-rich cases provided depth of understanding around the work of non-profit change agent leaders as well as supplied greater learning around issues that such leaders considered most important.

Non-profit organizations were chosen based on criteria that "[guide] identification of information-rich cases" to reflect the purpose of this study (Merriam and Tisdell 2016, 97). Initially, I gathered a general list of non-profit 501(c)(3) organizations from online directories such as www.guidestar.org as well as through personal networks. Subsequently, I chose organizations within the boundary of 501(c)(3) charitable and the like organizations that also included advocacy work on behalf of marginalized populations. Selected non-profits also had a social change mission aimed at improving the status quo for the sake of others. Characteristics such as combined local and global impact, headquartered in the United States, and established for at least five years were also prioritized.

One area of concern was people self-reporting as change agents without endorsement from another credible change agent. Three steps were taken to mitigate this risk. First, participants were also chosen based on recommendations from others as "change agents" rather than self-identification. Some initial participants were contacted based on my personal knowledge and recommendations from a personal connection at an organization that helps incubate change agents and entrepreneurs (detailed information about this organization is not shared to protect the anonymity of participants). From here, I continued to use a snowball method to ask participants for additional recommendations of change agents after the completion of each interview (Patton 2015, 298–301).

Second, the innovation literature informed the criteria for a change agent due to the overlap that exists between the change and innovation literatures (Mirvis 2017). In order to identity participants who were change agents, the following definition was contextually modified and used in communication with contacted organizations: A change agent works as a strategic communication link to facilitate the diffusion of new ideas to accomplish a social change mission (Rogers 2003, 368; Mirvis 2017; Komives, Wagner, and Associates 2017; Hill et al. 2014).

Third, in order to further guide participant identification, the following change agent roles were shared with the contacted organization or communicated to participants to generate snowball sampling: (1) a person who has a vision for change and thereby develops a need for change by bringing awareness to problems (Rogers 2003, 369–70; Borasi and Finnigan 2010); and (2) a person who consistently initiates and carries out new ideas (innovations) that add value to a change mission and to the clients being served (Borasi and Finnigan 2010).

Why Language Is Important

The terms in this book require clear definition in order to capture my intent in choosing specific language to describe the work of the non-profit sector and its leaders. This is especially important when researching non-profit organizations because "most definitions of the non-profit sector begin by stating what non-profit organizations are not and what they cannot do. Articulating what the non-profit sector is and does—and why—in positive terms is more difficult and requires more words" (Ott and Dicke 2016, 1).

Further, as previously stated, some overlap exists in the change and innovation literature (Mirvis 2017), which invites an integrated consideration with regards to their interrelationship in non-profit sector work. With full recognition that my chosen definition of terms may differ from those found in the existing literature and be understood differently based on context, the definitions that guide my study were chosen based on my intent to look through the lens of a change agent who is intentionally engaging in a social change mission for the common good.

Change Agent Leadership

Researchers study a variety of leadership styles that demand a need for clarity around the use of the word "leadership" (Anderson and Sun 2017). Inspired by the change and innovation research of Philip Mirvis (2017); Komives, Wagner, and Associates (2017); Linda Hill et al. (2014); and Everett M. Rogers (2003), I define the change agent as a leader who works as a strategic communication link to facilitate the diffusion of new ideas to accomplish a social change mission. This definition is considered especially relevant to the work of change agents who engage relationships across differences.[4]

Social Change

Building on the social change definition fundamental to the Social Change Model of Leadership Development,[5] the definition of social change is distinguished by the following attributes: (1) it is aimed at creating innovative change on behalf of others; (2) it addresses the root causes of social problems; (3) it is collaborative; (4) it requires new learning; and (5) it is not simple (Komives, Wagner, and Associates 2017). Last, social change is also conceptualized in the context of communicative processes that happen in relationships as a way to develop collective impact directed at disrupting and transforming dominant, exclusive, and/or violent social systems (adapted from Dutta 2011). Social change can take place both inside and outside the organization, especially when learning is required as part of the change process.

Social Innovation

I have chosen to use the definition provided by Stephanie Cosner Berzin, Humberto Camarena, and the European Commission's Guide to Social Innovation. First, Berzin and Camarena write that social innovation "can be thought of using three broad frameworks—shifting paradigms, creating action, and changing structures—it can also be imagined as a range of solutions that are now available to respond to social need. This range of solutions may cause change in paradigm, action, or structure or in multiple approaches at once" (2018, 11). Anheier, Krlev, and Mildenberger write that social innovation is "socially oriented and thus person-related" and "as a consequence of this person-centeredness, social innovation is fundamentally geared to serving social needs in unprecedented ways" (2019, 17). They also write: "Social innovations involve a higher degree of bottom up and grass-roots involvement ... . This can make their impact broader and more sustainable, but social innovations will typically take longer to evolve and sustain than other types of innovation. The most critical moderator will be their ability to gain legitimacy in a socially grounded negotiation process" (2019, 19).

Social Capital

Anheier, Krlev, and Mildenberger write: "Social capital describes the network of organizations and refers to the number and intensity of contacts of the organization to their stakeholders. It is also closely related to the level of trust which others ascribe to an organization as a result of or prerequisite for being embedded in such a network. Thus, social capital in this regard is not about the mere degree of closure and interaction but also about the intensity of embeddedness within a context" (2019, 267).

Collective Impact

The commitment of a group of important actors from different organizations (non-profit or for-profit) to a common agenda for solving a specific social problem. This definition is slightly modified from one provided by the Stanford Social Innovation Review, specifically in the Winter 2011 publication by John Kania and Mark Kramer.

Non-profit Social Change Organization

Underlying the use of this term is the assumption that non-profit organizations "exist to bring about a change in individuals and in society" (Drucker 1990, 3). Non-profit scholars provide several typologies for the study of non-profit organizations (Lewis, Hamel, and Richardson 2001; Salamon et al. 2013; Anheier 2014), but what is meant here by "non-profit organizations" are 501(c)(3) charitable and the like organizations that also participate in advocacy,[6] excluding church congregations and denominational agencies primarily to harness the scope of this study. These non-profit organizations have a social change mission that seeks to have a positive impact in the lives of the people as well as the social systems they serve. To encompass the relational aspects of my view of non-profit organizations, the phrase "non-profit social change organization" will be used in this study. It should be noted that there is a distinction in the literature between non-profit "social change" organizations versus non-profit "social service" organizations. The former focus on social change and innovation by disrupting the status quo whereas the latter focus mainly on providing service needs to different groups in society (Ospina and Foldy 2010; Anheier 2014; Ott and Dicke 2016). Although the lines between the two are blurry, with social change and service often intertwined, I have chosen to focus on non-profit social change organizations as officially named and described in the literature. In addition, the words "organization" and "institution" may be used interchangeably depending on the articles cited.

Community

Miroslav Volf describes community as an embrace rather than exclusion (1996), which is a description that works well in this study. Volf states that exclusion skews our perceptions of reality and causes us to react to others outside our personal relational circles with fear or anger. By contrast, an embrace of others requires us to open ourselves up to others in an effort to learn more about the reality of our interdependence.

Themes and Dimensions

The findings in this book are supported by diverse streams of research. I reviewed the precedent literature that connects non-profit sector work with social change and innovation. This was accomplished by building the foundation of non-profit social change work on the intersection of research that integrates the topics of communication and relationships. Specifically, the main theoretical frameworks on which my research rests include communication theory, relationship theory, educational theories of transformative and social learning, change theory, research in social innovation, and literature surrounding social entrepreneurship and intrapreneurship. These strands of literature provide a robust interdisciplinary framework that deepens our understanding of how non-profit change agents use relational communication strategies in their work.

My research found 12 themes that contribute to the literature and practice gaps. These 12 themes are presented as separate chapters and then discussed under the umbrella of three dimensions that enrich the understanding of the relational communication strategies of non-profit change agents. The first dimension is that non-profit change agents value people. Their high regard for people was not only the catalyst for their work, but also the foundation with which they approached their work. Oftentimes, change agents are seen as rash and harmfully disruptive to the status quo. However, the non-profit change agents in my research revealed that their respect for all people throughout all levels and stages of a change process caused them to wisely and strategically influence change as opportunities emerged. They did not force change on anyone or in any system but rather desired to partner with people if and when others wanted change.

Discerning these opportunities for change and key partnerships were critical to the non-profit change agents in my study, and they invested time and energy to plan well. Although they did not force change to happen, this should not be misunderstood as a passivity on behalf of the change agents. By contrast, non-profit change agents courageously acted upon their convictions to work for social change, but fully desired to value the dignity of people along the way to ultimately improve society for people in the end. They recognized that social change required a social process, which they valued just as much as the change itself.

The second dimension is that non-profit change agents value communication as process. Designing the process for change, from beginning to end, was important to the non-profit change agents in my study. Related to their value for people, non-profit change agents made sure that the change process included continued opportunities to learn through data collection and feedback loops, which required intentional conversations with different stakeholders. Oftentimes, they created and continued to shape organizational cultures where dialogue and open communication were valued as a way of working together. They were also intentional about creating conversations of accountability for others and for themselves so that the change process could move forward.

Finally, the third dimension is that non-profit change agents value change and embrace it as their purpose. This statement may seem unnecessary when talking about leaders who identify as change agents, but a distinction should be made that non-profit change agents did not state that they necessarily liked change. In fact, they frequently mentioned that change was uncomfortable and challenging, and required sacrifice. Despite this, non-profit change agents valued change for the potential of influencing life-giving outcomes for people. They were fully aware that in order to tackle some of the toughest social problems of our world, they needed to endure the challenges of change with hope for a better future for those they sought to serve.

Figure I.1 portrays the dialogue between the discerning change agent and the three dimensions of a change process. In this visual, people (the first dimension of relationships), process (the second dimension of communication), and purpose (the third dimension of change mission) are seen interacting with one another in a Venn diagram. What is not seen is the change agent, because change agents typically operate under the radar and prefer to be proximate to the people they serve. Therefore, one can assume that the change agent is within the people dimension. The overlapping spaces of the Venn diagram are areas in need of constant discernment by the change agent in order for him or her to more fully understand the layers of interaction. The movement toward the right represents the enduring interaction of the three dimensions throughout a change process, as well as the learning that occurs with continual discernment.

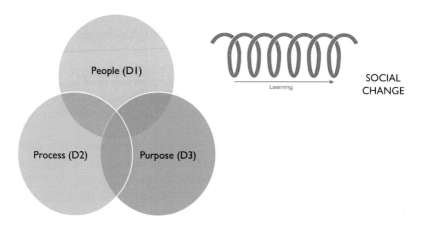

Figure I.1 Three Dimensions of Leading Change Well.

Overall, these three dimensions reveal a powerful interaction between communication and relationships that influence life-giving social change. These, along with the 12 themes found in my research, help deepen our understanding of the processes that are critical to catalyzing the need for, connecting people toward, and continuing momentum for a desired change. Specifically, this book bridges a gap in the literature on non-profit sector leadership by voicing the insights and concerns of change agent leaders who influence social change processes across diverse relational terrains. Voicing the experiences of non-profit change agents highlights the highly relational work in which they engage, which contributes guidance to other organizations as they adapt to an increasingly diverse workforce searching for meaningful, socially responsible work.

Audience

This book hopes to influence three distinct audiences. The first intended audience is those who identify as non-profit leaders, with the hope that this book can provide a platform for the voices of non-profit change agents as valued experts of change in their own right, a resource for learning and information sharing among the non-profit change agent community that seeks to serve others but is often not served in return, and an encouragement to continue the good work of social change and make a difference in our world. The second intended audience is the community of for-profit leaders. The hope is that this book may guide those who hold positions of authority in for-profit organizations, which often entail making hard decisions that impact people while simultaneously negotiating an organization's power dynamics. The findings in my study that concern co-creating processes that value the dignity of people, connecting people toward a new mission, or helping people learn how to change can be valuable to for-profit leaders who hold positions of authority that inherently require such interactions with people but could benefit from further wisdom. The third intended audience is leader developers, those who interact with emerging leaders who want to change the world. This audience could be educators, coaches, or mentors, for example, who have influence over emerging leaders, especially those who vocalize a desire to create new organizations, have new ideas, or impact society in some way. The hope is that this book can help prepare emerging change agents with a posture and awareness of change agent work that builds up the next generation of changemakers who are wise, discerning, humble, aware of self and others, respectful, and courageous.

One Final Note

I call myself a change agent. It is how I am naturally wired, and therefore is the primary lens I use when I enter into any sphere of influence. Initiating and sustaining change through relationships and strategic communication on behalf of others is my core passion and vocational calling. This passion emerged from my childhood when I experienced racism and marginalization as an Asian–American female growing up in a homogenous environment that centered whiteness. Ever since, I have wanted to change systems and structures for myself and others who experience marginalization. I have worked in non-profit organizations for over 20 years creating, re-building, or revitalizing systems and structures. Therefore, I have an idea of what successful change processes look like since I have both led change and seen the fruit of such experiences. However, I am still learning and growing into the change agent role and anticipate wisdom from you to inform my own thinking and practice as you read and interact with this book.

Notes

1 First described in 1985 by economists and university professors Warren Bennis and Burt Nanus in their book *Leaders: The Strategies for Taking Charge*, VUCA helps describe the challenges posed to leaders by various external factors.
2 With the exception of The Leadership Quarterly's special 1994 issue on social change leadership.
3 My definition of social change builds on the social change definition fundamental to the Social Change Model of Leadership Development created by Komives, Wagner, and Associates 2017.

4 "Difference" refers to any socially defined marker that exists to separate one person from another and that can also be used to de-value the other. Examples include gender, race, and socioeconomic status.
5 This model states that social change is distinguished by the following attributes: (1) it is aimed at creating change; (2) it addresses the root causes of social problems; (3) it is collaborative; and (4) it is not simple (Komives, Wagner, and Associates 2017, 235–236).
6 Advocacy organizations "promote social, economic, and/or political causes and include political parties, citizen groups, and lobbying groups among others" (Lewis, Hamel, and Richardson 2001, 8).

References

Adair, John. 2002. *Effective Strategic Leadership*. London: Macmillan.
Almog-Bar, M. and Schmid, H. 2014. "Advocacy Activities of Nonprofit Human Service Organizations: A Critical Review." *Nonprofit and Voluntary Sector Quarterly* 43, no. 1: 11–35.
Anderson, Marc H. and Sun, Peter Y.T. 2017. "Reviewing Leadership Styles: Overlaps and the Need for a New 'Full-Range' Theory." *International Journal of Management Reviews* 19: 76–96.
Anheier, Helmut K. 2014. *Nonprofit Organizations: Theory, Management, Policy*. New York, NY: Routledge.
Anheier, Helmut K., Krlev, Gorgi, and Mildenberger, Georg. 2019. *Social Innovation: Comparative Perspectives*. New York, NY: Routledge.
Baer, Linda L., Duin, Ann H., and Bushway, Deborah. 2015. "Change Agent Leadership." *Planning for Higher Education Journal* 43, no. 3: 1–11.
Bennis, Warren and Nanus, Burt. 2004. *Leaders*. New York: Harper Collins.
Berzin, Stephanie Cosner and Camarena, Humberto. 2018. *Innovation from Within*. New York, NY: Oxford University Press.
Borasi, Raffaella, and Finnigan, Kara. 2010. "Entrepreneurial Attitudes and Behaviors That Can Help Prepare Successful Change Agents in Education." *The New Educator* 6: 1–29.
Boyd, A.S. and Wilmoth, M.C. 2006. "An Innovative Community-Based Intervention for African American Women with Breast Cancer: The Witness Project." *Health and Social Work* 31, no. 1: 77–80.
Brothers, John and Sherman, Anne. 2012. *Building Nonprofit Capacity: A Guide to Managing Change Through Organizational Lifecycles*. San Francisco, CA: Jossey-Bass.
Buono, Anthony F. and Kerber, Kenneth W. 2010. "Creating a Sustainable Approach to Change: Building Organizational Change Capacity." *SAM Advanced Management Journal* 75, no. 2: 4–14, 21.
Burnes, B. 2004. "Kurt Lewin and the Planned Approach to Change: A Re-Appraisal." *Journal of Management Studies* 41: 977–1002.
Child, C. and Gronbjerg, K. 2007. "Nonprofit Advocacy Organizations: Their Characteristics and Activities." *Social Science Quarterly* 88, no. 1: 259–281.
Colvin, G. 2000. "Managing in the Info Era." *Fortune* 141, no. 5: F6–F9.
Colwill, Deborah A. 2021. *Conflict, Power, and Organizational Change*. New York, NY: Routledge.

Cummings, Thomas G. and Worley, Christopher G. 2015. *Organization Development and Change*. Stamford, CT: Cengage Learning.

Drucker, Peter F. 1990. *Managing the Nonprofit Organization*. New York, NY: HarperCollins Publishers.

Dutta, Mohan J. 2011. *Communicating Social Change*. New York, NY: Routledge.

Florin, P., Chavis, D.M., Wandersman, A., and Rich, R. 1992. "A Systems Approach to Understanding and Enhancing Grassroots Organizations: The Block Booster Project." In *Analysis of Dynamic Psychological Systems*, edited by R. Levine and H. Fitzgerald, Vol. 2, pp. 215–243. New York: Plenum.

Hailey, J. and James, R. 2004. "Trees Die from the Top: International Perspectives on NGO Leadership Development." *International Journal of Voluntary and Nonprofit Organizations* 15, no. 4: 343–353.

Higgs, Malcolm and Rowland, D. 2005. "All Changes Great and Small: Exploring Approaches to Change and its Leadership." *Journal of Change Management* 5, no. 2: 121–151, 10.1080/14697010500082902

Higgs, Malcolm and Rowland, Deborah. 2010. "Emperors with Clothes On: The Role of Self-Awareness in Developing Effective Change Leadership." *Journal of Change Management* 10, no. 4: 369–385.

Hill, Linda A., Brandeau, Greg, Truelove, Emily, and Lineback, Kent. 2014. *Collective Genius*. Boston, MA: Harvard Business School Publishing.

Hinrichs, Gina and Richardson, Cheryl B. 2015. *Large Scale Change for Non-Profits: A Playbook for Social Sector Capacity Building*. Charlotte, NC: Information Age Publishing, Inc.

Jaskyte, K. 2004. "Transformational Leadership, Organizational Culture, and Innovativeness in Nonprofit Organizations." *Nonprofit Management and Leadership* 15, no. 2: 153–168.

Kania, John and Kramer, Mark. 2011. "Collective Impact." *Stanford Social Innovation Review*. www.ssireview.org

Keller, Scott and Aiken, C. 2008. "The Inconvenient Truth about Change Management." *McKinsey and Company*. https://www.aascu.org/corporate-partnership/McKinseyReport2.pdf

Kerber, Kenneth W. and Anthony F. Buono. 2018. "In Defense of Directed Change: A Viable Approach in the Rhythm of Change." Academy of Management Proceedings 2018, no. 1. Briarcliff Manor, NY: Academy of Management.

Kimberlin, S.E. 2010. "Advocacy by Nonprofits: Roles and Practices of Core Advocacy Organizations and Direct Service Organizations." *Journal of Policy Practice* 9: 164–182.

Komives, Susan R., Wagner, Wendy, and Associates. 2017. *Leadership for a Better World*. San Francisco, CA: John Wiley & Sons.

Kotter, John. 1995. https://hbr.org/1995/05/leading-change-why-transformation-efforts-fail-2

Kotter, J. 1996. *Leading Change*. Cambridge, MA: Harvard Business School Press.

Lewis, Laurie K., Hamel, Stephanie A., and Richardson, Brian K. 2001. "Communicating Change to Nonprofit Stakeholders: Models and Predictors of Implementors' Approaches." *Management Communication Quarterly* 15, no. 5: 5–41.

McDonald, R.E. 2007. "An Investigation of Innovation in Nonprofit Organizations: The Role of Organizational Mission." *Nonprofit and Voluntary Quarterly* 36: 256–281.

Mellinger, M.S. 2014. "Beyond Legislative Advocacy: Exploring Agency, Legal, and Community Advocacy." *Journal of Policy Practice* 13, no. 1: 45–58.

Merriam, Sharan B. and Tisdell, Elizabeth J. 2016. *Qualitative Research*. San Francisco, CA: Jossey-Bass.

Miller, David. 2001. "Successful Change Leaders: What Makes Them? What Do They Do That Is Different?" *Journal of Change Management* 2, no. 4: 359–368, 10.1080/714042515

Mirvis, Philip. 2017. "Redesigning Business to Serve Society: Joining Organization Development and Social Innovation." *OD Practitioner* 49, no. 3: 30–38.

Mosley, J.E. and Ros, A. 2011. "Nonprofit Agencies in Public Child Welfare: Their Role and Involvement in Policy Advocacy." *Journal of Public Child Welfare* 5: 297–317.

Ospina, Sonia and Foldy, Erica. 2010. "Building Bridges from the Margins: The Work of Leadership in Social Change Organizations." *The Leadership Quarterly* 21: 292–307.

Ott, Steven J. and Dicke, Lisa A. 2016. *The Nonprofit Sector*. Boulder, CO: Westview Press.

Patton, M.Q. 2015. *Qualitative Research and Evaluation Methods (4th ed.)*. Thousand Oaks, CA: Sage.

Perkins, Douglas D., Bess, Kimberly D., Cooper, Daniel G., Jones, Diana L., Armstead, Theresa, and Speer, Paul W. 2007. "Community Organizational Learning: Case Studies Illustrating a Three-Dimensional Model of Levels and Orders of Change." *Journal of Community Psychology* 35, no. 3: 303–328.

Rogers, Everett M. 2003. *Diffusion of Innovations (5th edition)*. New York, NY: Free Press.

Ruben, Brent D. and Gigliotti, Ralph A. 2016. "Leadership as Social Influence: An Expanded View of Leadership Communication Theory and Practice." *Journal of Leadership and Organizational Studies* 23, no. 4: 467–479.

Ruben, B.D. and Stewart, L. 2016. *Communication and Human Behavior (6th ed.)*. Dubuque, IA: Kendall Hunt.

Salamon, Lester M., Sokolowski, Wojciech, Haddock, Megan A., and Tice, Helen S. 2013. *The State of Global Civil Society and Volunteering: Latest Findings from the Implementation of the UN Nonprofit Handbook*. Working Paper No. 49. Baltimore: Johns Hopkins Center for Civil Society Studies.

Schmid, H., Bar, M., and Nirel, R. 2008. "Advocacy Activities in Nonprofit Human Service Organizations: Implications for Policy." *Nonprofit and Voluntary Sector Quarterly* 37, no. 4: 581–602.

Shier, M.L. and Graham, J.R. 2013. "Identifying Social Service Needs of Muslims Living in a Post 9/11 Era: The Role of Community-Based Organizations." *Advances in Social Work* 14, no. 2: 379–394.

Shier, M.L., McDougle, L.M., and Handy, F. 2014. "Nonprofits and the Promotion of Civic Engagement: A Conceptual Framework for Understanding the 'Civic Footprint' of Nonprofits within Local Communities." *The Canadian Journal of Nonprofit and Social Economy Research* 5, no. 1: 57–75.

Smollan, Roy K., Sayers, J.G., and Matheny, J. 2010. "Emotional Responses to the Speed, Frequency, and Timing of Organizational Change." *Time and Society* 19, no. 1: 28–53.

Spergel, I.A. and Grossman, S.F. 1997. "The Little Village Project: A Community Approach to the Gang Problem." *Social Work* 42, no. 5: 456–470.

Stroh, David Peter. 2015. *Systems Thinking for Social Change*. White River Junction, VT: Chelsea Green Publishing.

Thompson, Janice L. 2002. "The World of the Social Entrepreneur." *International Journal of Public Sector Management* 15, no. 5: 412–431.

Uhl-Bien, M., Marion, R., and McKelvey, B. 2007. "Complexity Leadership Theory: Shifting Leadership from the Industrial Age to the Knowledge Era." *The Leadership Quarterly* 18, no. 4: 298–318.

Van de Ven, Andrew H. and Sun, Kangyong. 2011. "Breakdowns in Implementing Models of Organization Change." *Academy of Management Perspectives* 25, no. 3: 58–74.

Van Loon, Rens. 2017. *Creating Organizational Value through Dialogical Leadership*. Tilburg, The Netherlands: Springer.

Volf, Miroslav. 1996. *Exclusion and Embrace: A Theological Exploration of Identity, Otherness, and Reconciliation*. Nashville, TN: Abingdon Press.

Weerawardena, Jay, McDonald, Robert E., and Mort, Gillian Sullivan. 2010. "Sustainability of Nonprofit Organizations: An Empirical Investigation." *Journal of World Business* 45: 346–356.

Weerawardena, Jay and Mort, Gillian Sullivan. 2012. "Competitive Strategy in Socially Entrepreneurial Nonprofit Organizations: Innovation and Differentiation." *American Marketing Association* 31, no. 1: 91–101.

Chapter 1

Context: The Who, Why, and Where of Change Leaders

Growing up in the 90s as a Korean–American female in Salt Lake City, Utah was disorienting, to say the least. I experienced marginalization and anti-Asian racism throughout my teenage years, which expressed themselves in more subtle yet still profoundly similar ways within the organizations in which I eventually worked. Painful experiences like these shaped my conviction to partner with others to "change the world" so we could all experience more dignity and flourishing. Personal testimonies like this also emerged from my interviews with non-profit change agents. They are testimonies of real personal experiences that cultivated genuine purpose and passion for change for the sake of others. As change leaders, when our lived experiences converge with the reason why we lead change, we begin to lead change with greater integrity and wisdom.

Change leaders who value human dignity understand that their role in leading change not only has implications that could change the lives of generations, but also that they themselves are implicated in both the problems and solutions they engage. This chapter first paints a picture of the major experiences that influenced leaders' convictions to become change agents within the non-profit sector. All of their experiences were varied but pivotal. Their reflections showcase the unique backgrounds that shaped a rare range of skills within these change agent leaders, as well as the depth of their passion not only for the human race, but also for a more just and equitable world. After presenting a summary of factors that influenced their full immersion into change agent work, I will place these leaders within the backdrop of the non-profit sector by providing a brief balcony view of their broader context.

Personal Context

"We don't see the world as it is, we see it as we are."—Anaïs Nin

The truth in this quote from Anaïs Nin is captured in the personal stories of non-profit change leaders interviewed in this book. Their

DOI: 10.4324/9781003272243-2

stories testify of the power of proximate and personal experiences to shape our view of ourselves, others, and the world around us. Their stories also reveal different kinds of soil that helped cultivate conviction and passion to lead change with and for others.

The Soil of Upbringing

Many change leaders mentioned that family life was a major influence in seeding their convictions for social change. For example, one change leader shared that growing up on a farm shaped her problem-solving skills and her ability to discern disharmony:

> On the farm, everybody works together. My dad was crippled and he had this season where he couldn't farm. And so, the community showed up with their combines, all the neighbors, and did it for him. We come together with all our combines and plows. Then, when I go to other contexts it's almost shocking how broken community life can be and I think: "Wow, something's wrong here." I think my ability to see what's missing and offer solutions has to do with an upbringing that—not that my upbringing was always harmonious—helps me sense when things aren't right here and we could work together to make them right.

Another change leader also reflected on her upbringing and shared that observing her parents in ministry influenced her heart to serve others:

> I grew up in Kentucky and we didn't have a lot of money, but my parents served in ministry and I think that was very influential. My dad was a chaplain in the back side of a race track in Kentucky. And so, as little kids we would walk around with him on the back side of a race track and minister to folks who make no money in the race horse industry; to those who take care of the horses and are kind of on the low end of the totem pole so to speak. We would do these Wednesday night services in the chapel and my job was to set up the chairs and put the hymn books on the chairs. And I just remember that example of my parents who were serving in that area. And then we moved to South Eastern Kentucky where my dad became a mountain preacher. Again, as a kid, I just tagged along in that. And I think that's kind of where my passion to serve others started.

Similarly, another change leader talked about how her family influenced her life and vocational choices:

> I come from a long line of social workers. My mother worked for the State of Illinois for thirty years. So, growing up, I would go to her

office, help her file things, and listen to her talk about policy and policy changes and things like that. Also, my aunt worked for the Department of Child and Family Services. I have always had this strong group of women who have worked in social services. So, when I went to college, I knew I wanted to be in public relations, but I also knew that I wanted to work in a social impact field and the non-profit sector. Ever since, I've looked for ways to marry those two loves.

In addition, one change leader expressed that traveling with her family when she was a child opened her eyes to the discrepancies that exist in the world:

I was born and raised in Dubai and every summer I would travel to India to visit extended family where I was exposed to extreme poverty and the severity of the discrepancies in the world. Through these summer trips, I recognized there was a huge difference between how people lived. And that's always been with me. As I got older, I got involved in a bunch of non-profit organizations and volunteered with whatever I could to work towards the solution for those living in poverty-stricken conditions.

The Soil of Faith

All change leaders who identified as Christian talked about their engagement with social change work as one major way to express their love for God. They felt a distinct calling from God to become a social change agent and many mentioned their faith and hope in God helped them persevere during challenging times. For example, one Christian change leader said:

I just knew that I loved the Lord and I knew that I wanted to serve him and serve youth in at-risk areas or underserved places. So, for me, it's about the calling God placed on my life and wherever God took me was fine with me—in my current season, that happens to be in a non-profit. This is just what God's called me to do.

Another also shared how God directed his steps toward opportunities so he could become the change agent he felt convicted to be.

I grew up in Chinatown, which is a neighborhood here in Chicago. I went through high school and really became convicted about my faith in college. I was ready to go into full-time ministry work. There was a

Christian organization that I always thought would be fun to work in, but my parents being Asian parents really just said, "Look, you know you're going to be a doctor or an engineer or lawyer so you better go pick one." And so, honestly that's really how I started my political career. I actually just decided to go to law school and took an internship at the governor's office. From there, one thing led to another and I eventually found myself in Washington working at the White House. I ran for a congressional seat. And, I think it was during that time when I had this nudging feeling that maybe I should leave my job to go do something that was more impactful. And I think it was during that time when I was convicted that as a child of God, because God is a creator, everything I create should in fact actually be honoring to God even in the work I do. So, it doesn't mean that I leave my job in order to pursue something that I deem to be more holy. But rather, the question I asked myself was, "How do I do what I'm doing and have that be honoring to God?" God opened some doors where I was able to work with a lot of international Christian ministries helping them build their capacity. And now I lead an organization that focuses solely on doing this work.

Similarly, another Christian change leader passionately expressed God's movement in her life:

I was president of an ad agency and in 1997, through prayer, God birthed a vision in my heart and mind based on John 10:10—the thief comes to steal, kill, and destroy, I have come that you may have life and have it abundantly. I clearly understood that God wanted my life to be about helping kids in Chicago have abundant life. So, I continued working in advertising while volunteering with kids through a local church at night and on the weekends. In 2001, I left advertising and started this organization with sixteen kids who lived in Cabrini-Green [a neighborhood on the north side of Chicago]. In 2005, we became a separate 501c3. And today we serve 1,523 kids in four different neighborhoods in five sites, soon to be six sites.

Also, one Christian change leader talked about the tension of discerning God's leading in his life:

In college I had a vision of a purpose inspired by faith, but the path that was unfolding in front of me was business. So, I felt that tension for a long time but entered business and was really fortunate to work for a couple of Fortune 500 companies that took me through management development programs and paid for some master's work. However, there was always this tug back towards that initial vision and greater purpose of meaningfully impacting the lives of those around me. I started living into this greater purpose in very simple ways by volunteering or starting different initiatives. I assembled a group of 300–500 people and led a trip down to help rebuild New Orleans after [Hurricane] Katrina. And on the way back I had a very clear understanding from God that God wired me to create infrastructure for others to get involved in large-scale social issues.

Likewise, another Christian change leader voiced his belief that God had wired him in a specific way to be a change agent:

My wife and I were on staff with a missions organization and part of how God has wired us is to be a little more of the pioneering, entrepreneurial type. And we understood pretty early on that our gifts and strengths and skills were a little more entrepreneurial. So, the missions organization would consistently send us to start some new things, and they had asked us to go to India to do work amongst some of the influencers within the Indian culture to try and figure out how to bring about social change socioeconomically from the top down.

The Soil of Pivotal Experiences

Several change leaders communicated that disorienting or challenging life experiences influenced their decision to become a change agent in the non-profit sector. For instance, one leader shared that the death of his father and grandmother on the same day influenced reflection that changed the trajectory of his career:

Well, it starts with a personal story. I was in the golf business. I ran golf schools for Golf Digest. My dad and my grandmother died on the same day. I think I mention that for two reasons. One, it was a big pivotal moment in my life obviously, and then it also made me reflect on my life and whether I was simply successful or if I was actually significant, and there's a big difference between the two. I decided to leave the golf business thinking I was going to be an elementary school teacher in an at-risk school. I spent two years as a reading paraprofessional working with struggling students. As I taught students how to read, I saw their excitement and hope; I was convicted that literacy is the most important skill any of us will ever have. So, I started a non-profit to tackle the social issue of illiteracy.

Similarly, another leader shared a pivotal experience in her life that influenced the ways in which she wanted to contribute to the world:

I studied international relations in college and my intent behind that was to do development work. Through some of the opportunities I had as a student to go to Central America, I saw on the ground community development work through a concrete project. For example, we built a water system that brought the community together and helped identify formal and informal local leadership. I wondered what other progress could be made through one concrete thing that unified people. I was really interested in thinking about immediate relief in combination with long-term development. So, I eventually took a job in Chicago working with refugee families, and that was a pivotal change, which made me think more about what it meant to be part of the majority culture wrestling with questions of development and progress rather than transplanting myself into another country where I had no idea what the social structures were, how things happened, etc. All of this was a turning point in how I understood economic development. With a new mindset, I started the organization I currently lead in partnership with a church on the south side of Chicago that had a mission to make an impact in the field of economic development.

Another leader talked about the diversity of challenges in his life that propelled him into change agent work:

My dad left when I was four. Divorce and separation at that time was unheard of so my family and I were ostracized. I remember when I was four or five, when my mom wasn't educated at that time. She didn't have a job. We didn't have a car. We were foreclosing on the house. I remember opening up the pantry and there being no food. At that moment, I said, "I'm never gonna be hungry again and I'm going to be in control." Fast forward to the age of twenty-eight, I was struck ill on one of my work trips. Thought I had the flu. They discovered I had large holes in the lower right lobe of my lung. And so, I ended up having a portion of my lung removed. Everything since then got like this [makes hand motion of turning something upside down]. I got laid off. Jobless, I was invited to a fundraising event to give to an organization that served marginalized teenagers. I'd never been to a fundraiser, but I remember cutting the biggest check I ever cut, and I asked if they needed any help and they were like, "We're leaving for camp tomorrow and we're short one male counselor." Accepting this invitation changed everything. Now I oversee an organization that serves marginalized urban youth.

The Soil of Unintentional Transition

Some change leaders communicated that their entry into the non-profit sector was unintentional, but the non-profit sector "found" them simply after they acted upon their passion to serve others. Specifically, one leader shared this very journey:

> Definitely didn't mean to. I was teaching at a school on the southwest side of Chicago. It's a school that became well known for the violence in the neighborhood and the poverty surrounding it. I started teaching there in 2008 and at the same time, the person who turned out to be my cofounder started teaching there too. During our time there, we started taking our students on different experiences outside the classroom. At the time we were told by people that we shouldn't take these students places because we don't know what they're going do outside the school walls. Our immersive experiences were so well-liked by students that we created a more permanent after-school program and saw that students' GPA[s] and their test scores were making faster gains than the rest of the school. We expanded our after-school program to three other schools while still teaching. And at that point we knew we had to incorporate and start raising money because we had been doing this out of our pockets. So, I did not intend to get into non-profit work—it kind of found me.

Another leader also mentioned that he just happened to enter into the non-profit sector:

> I think when I started, I didn't even fully grasp exactly what a not for profit was. I was really just trying to innovate and solve a problem I perceived around high abortion rates. So, my wife and I, instead of buying a house, we basically got married and bought a Mercedes Sprinter van that was gutted, moved into it, drove the country to music festivals, and cast a vision of what we wanted to do. It was pure misery for several years. We launched the first pro-life bus at the end of 2013, and we were able to reach and compel 394 women to make a decision for life who were previously choosing an abortion. That's when it took off. My non-profit was an overnight success after that.

The Soil of Education

Some leaders shared that educational experiences influenced their desire to enter into change agent work. For example, one leader reflected on how the information to which he was exposed in graduate school influenced his conviction to become a change agent:

> In graduate school, I took an urban anthropology class and felt my heart drawn to the city and to the injustices that were there. I had grown up feeling an ache around racial and economic justice having moved to a neighborhood that had some racial segregation and issues surrounding that, but never really knowing what I could do about it. In class, I learned about people moving into lower income communities and being part of what was going on in there and partnering up with local organizations and leaders who were bringing about change. It just connected deeply with what my heart had been longing for. By the end of my time in graduate school, I had honed in on wanting to work for either a community-organizing organization or an urban mission organization.

Another leader also reflected on the strong influence of her educational journey:

> I have an undergrad degree in international relations and a minor in economics. I also did a third one in race and critical theory. My educational institution got me thinking about the world around us and it helped me think about my observations, perspectives, and experiences in the world. This catalyzed thinking about very particular ways in which I could be helpful in leading change. So, I participated in a program at a university where I lived in East Africa for a year to do a short internship with the UN in a refugee camp. Even through my undergrad years, I noticed one thing that was definitely missing—a gendered perspective on all of the issues I had been looking at. Even my race and critical theory classes were heavily taught by male professors. Thus, I had adopted a male perspective around the experience of racism and oppression. I was always looking for the perspective from women and where women fit in as change leaders and so I started working with this group called Gender Sensitive Initiative run by a Kenyan anthropologist woman. This opportunity began my work looking specifically at gender issues around community development.

Further, another leader shared a similar story:

> I went to a liberal arts school, and the president of [a social change organization] came and presented the concept of social change in a way that was just really attractive. I was already interested in making some kind of social impact in my future work, and I had done some

overseas stuff, but hearing the speaker say, "You don't have to go far away to make a social impact. It's right in your backyard" was both new and enlightening. So, I applied to his social change organization and I moved to Philly for a year and then have basically been with the organization ever since.

The Soil of Discontent

Many change leaders expressed their discontent with the social problems that exist in the world. Their discontent influenced them deeply, to the point where they felt they could no longer ignore their burdens to contribute to social change. One change leader shared his discontent with how the Korean-led church created generational trauma, which is what he had known all his life, and his burning desire to change that for others:

> I felt like I was in a box. I remember praying and saying, "God, if there's a different paradigm for ministry that's outside the Korean church, I want to learn it and I don't care where it is. I don't care if it's a white church, black church, Hispanic church. I just have to see what else is out there." I couldn't ignore it any longer. And so, while I was in New York, I sent out my résumé to all these churches I thought were doing innovative things that were outside the box to learn how I could bring fresh, new ideas to the institution of the Church. Eventually, I began working for a non-profit that seeks to change the paradigm for how churches operate across the world.

In addition, another change leader mentioned a time when she experienced discontent that led to a career pivot into the work of leading change to impact lives differently:

> My background is in film production, and I wanted to make a film about women who had overcome tremendous obstacles and were inspiring hope in their communities. Being a Chinese American woman, I was very aware of media misrepresentation of women of color, especially of the Global South, and how a lot of women were depicted as people who were starving, dying in war and helpless. And so, I wanted to reframe that narrative by finding stories of women who, despite tremendous obstacles, were actually leaders and impacting communities. My first film project was in Kenya, but during the process of making the film I was confronted with a lot of stories of sexual violence. I was hearing story after story of trauma upon trauma and how sexual violence was directly related

to lack of access to education, especially for younger. I came home, made the film, started touring with the film, and in the process of touring with the film, I just realized that the film wasn't enough. That the film, though it might provide education and awareness, did not tangibly do anything for the community of survivors I was meeting and building relationships with. So, I switched careers and built a non-profit specifically for the survivors who were my friends and our mission was created from their hopes and dreams of how they wanted to use education to build better leadership in their communities.

Moreover, another change leader's unsettling experiences serving his local community propelled him to start his organization:

I volunteered at a local church where we gave people meals and set up shelter within the church building for those who needed it. So many people had needs, so I worked with the church and community leaders to make the church building an official site to serve the homeless community. I really became quite moved by seeing home-less families come in, especially single women with children. What was unsettling was everyone slept in a big single room within the church building. So over on one side you've got all these guys with whatever problems brought them there for the evening, whether addictions, mental health issues, loss of a job, etc. And over on the other side, you've got eight-year-old girls sleeping. That's not quite right. So, I started asking myself some questions: What are we supposed to do about that? What am I supposed to do? That's how I started my non-profit organization.

Further, another change leader talked about a time when he was angered by a man who oversaw an organization that hired sex slaves:

In an effort to solve the problem of human trafficking, I travelled across the world to learn from anyone I could. One day, I ended up talking to a pimp who complained about the young women he hired for his business. I remember being angered by his audacity and arrogance while literally banking on the abuse of these young women. And he was so confident that no one could shut his business down. I started to wrestle with the reality of whether or not that was true. Are we not willing to really step in and do what it takes to bring about change for women in this situation? Am I willing? That wrestling match with myself led to the birth of my non-profit organization.

The Soil of Invitation

Finally, several change leaders expressed they were invited by others into change leadership work and the non-profit sector based upon their proven skills and abilities. For example, one leader said:

> A prominent Black leader in the Chicagoland area reached out to me and said, "Hey, I got this idea to help bring urban renewal and dignity, and reduce violence and poverty in Chicago. My idea involves manufacturing and since you're a manufacturing CEO, let me buy you breakfast. I want to run my idea by you." After breakfast, he said—"You should lead this."

Likewise, another change leader mentioned:

> I was invited to initially join an international non-profit organization doing social change work around human trafficking. I really enjoyed that. It was also very technical and very specific. Then, I was invited to consider a position at my current organization, which would give me a broader sandbox to work on social change issues I cared about, including human trafficking. Now I'm the Executive Director of this organization.

Another change leader was also sought out and invited into the work she does today:

> I first started working with a world-renowned consultant. He asked me to work as a consultant with him for twelve years. Then, my current organization approached me several years ago and asked me if I would be interested in putting my hat in the ring. Initially, I said no. However, in their relentless pursuit, I eventually became more intrigued and made the official transition to become their Executive Director.

Finally, another change leader explained:

> So how I got this job is I had been in academia at a law school. I was running a program at a think tank, and then I had left that job because I really wanted to be more hands-on and more of an advocate. I transitioned to consulting for some national nonprofits and one of the staff emailed me a job description to consider. I knew one of the board members of this particular non-profit organization so I called her and said, "I'm not really sure it's the right thing for me because I have mainly done national work. This is more local." She replied, "Oh no, I

think that'd be really interesting. You should definitely apply." So, I applied! That's how I became ED [Executive Director].

The personal stories above summarize how the change agents interviewed for this book were shaped for the work of change and the challenges that accompany it. Their testimonies illuminate several characteristics of change agents and their work that invite attention. First, change agents were aware of the problems that existed and willingly chose to solve them. Second, change agents understood their life experiences, both good and challenging, as preparation to solve social problems in their contexts. Last, the work of change demanded change agents be adaptable and agile in order to solve social problems. These unique characteristics provide a contextual launching point toward understanding the types of change leaders centered in this book.

Public Context

Stated previously and evident in their personal stories, the work of change demands change agents be adaptable and agile in order to solve complex social problems in our ever-changing world. In the following chapters, we'll review the broader context in which these leaders operate and how their context also demands specific skills for maximum impact.

We live in a rapidly changing world where organizations constantly manage the intersection of diversity and the global expansion of organizational functioning that result in everyday negotiations of divergent values and ways of seeing the world (Hersted and Gergen 2013; Fry 2021). Additionally, organizations' more recent focus on efforts to contain COVID-19, address racial injustice, and productively engage conversations in our increasingly tribal culture contributes layers of profound dislocation for organizational leaders and company cultures (Spicer 2020; Hecht 2020). Given these disorienting realities, how can we lead change that is people-centric and advances the flourishing of others?

The non-profit sector and its leaders can provide an important context for learning how to lead change differently. Non-profit organizations are created to solve some of the most complex social problems in our world (Berzin and Camarena 2018). Reframing challenges as opportunities, the non-profit sector helps shape society and lead innovative social change inside organizations, within their surrounding communities, and across the globe (Weerawardena, McDonald, and Mort 2010; Anheier, Krlev, and Mildenberger 2019). It is important to pause and clarify how the term social change is defined for the purposes of this research. Building on the social change definition fundamental to the Social Change Model of Leadership Development,[1] the definition of social change is distinguished by the following attributes: (1) it is aimed at creating innovative change on behalf of others; (2) it addresses the root causes of social problems; (3) it is collaborative; (4) it requires new learning; and (5) it is not simple (Komives, Wagner, and Associates 2017). Last, social change is also conceptualized in the context of communicative processes that happen in relationships as a way to develop collective impact directed at disrupting and transforming dominant, exclusive, and/or violent social systems (adapted from Dutta 2011). Social change can take place both inside and outside the organization, especially when learning is required as part of the change process. Couched in this definition, leading social change not only seeks to improve the human condition and society in a new way, but also values the process of "how people engage with each other" to accomplish the change mission (Komives, Wagner, and Associates 2017, 2).

Peter Drucker writes, "The non-profit organization exists to bring about a change in individuals and society" (1990, 3). Based on the IRS business master file of tax-exempt organizations,[2] there are more than 20 different categories of non-profit organizations that include an expansive array of entities (Roeger et al. 2012). This master file also reveals that the 501 (c)(3) (religious, charitable, and similar) and 501 (c)(4) (civic leagues and social welfare) organizations account for more than three-quarters of all non-profit organizations (Roeger et al. 2012). Understandably, then, when referencing the non-profit sector, people tend to speak simply of organizations, foundations, and associations (Anheier 2014). However, to speak of the non-profit sector comprehensively includes also reflecting on the values and motivations that drive non-profit sector activities such as philanthropy, civic engagement, social capital, and social entrepreneurship (Anheier 2014; Ott and Dicke 2016).[3]

Research suggests non-profits influence social change in multiple ways (Shier and Graham 2013; Shier et al. 2014; Shier and Handy 2015). Non-profit organizations engage in unplanned change occurrences as well as deliberate change strategies in response to the complexity of problems they face in our post-industrial world (Brothers and Sherman 2012; Hinrichs and Richardson 2015). With change happening at a pace markedly faster than in a more stable industrial world, non-profit organizations are moving toward problem-solving models that allow organizations to be more agile in their responses (Hinrichs and Richardson 2015). Leaders of non-profit organizations also conduct their work in a "post-bureaucratic" world where organizations are characterized by less hierarchy, increased boundary-less collaboration, and greater opportunities for information-sharing between departments and across sectors (Mirvis 2017).

Leaders of non-profit social change organizations are "human-change agents" (Drucker 1990, 112) who need unique skills that differ from those of their for-profit counterparts (Phipps and Burbach 2010). Specifically, non-profit leaders develop organizational learning capacity through greater attention to communications and therefore fill "informational roles" that are not necessarily top priority for for-profit executives (Gill 2010; Taliento and Silverman 2005; Dargie 1998). In his book *Managing the Nonprofit Organization*, Drucker states, "The most important do is to build the organization around information and communication instead of around hierarchy" (1990, 115). With the demand for non-profit leaders to engage multiple and diverse stakeholders in the change and learning process, non-profit social change leaders function as conveners and facilitate an environment that strengthens the interdependence between communication, collective thinking, and the learning that happens through relationships.

Facilitating a strong relational ecosystem is also important to the non-profit leader's ability to foster innovation. Non-profits focused on a social change mission require innovation as much as businesses or other government entities (Drucker 1990; McDonald 2007). The capacity to innovate is important to a non-profit's long-term sustainability (Phipps and Burbach 2010) because innovative non-profits are better positioned to adapt to future demands as well as to anticipate future opportunities for growth (Kanter and Summers 1987). Non-profit innovation depends on the leader's ability to prepare the organization for possible crises that result in generative outcomes (i.e. innovation), thereby developing an organizational culture and practice of innovation (Light 1998). A real limitation for non-profits, however, is that non-profit leaders build and develop their organizations with limited resources that can distract from or even hinder missional goals, employee training (Phipps and Burbach 2010), and thus, the innovation needed to survive and thrive.

Given this background, the emergence of complex problems that demand quick learning and responsiveness combined with increased relational interaction can pressure leaders with noble large-scale intentions to attempt change strategies as individuals rather than in concert with others (Hassan 2014). According to David Peter Stroh, there are four common challenges of change: (1) motivation (Why should we change?); (2) collaboration (Why should we work together?); (3) focus (What should we do?); and (4) learning (Why bother?) (Stroh 2015). Given the difficult change journey, non-profit change agents need to engage others with both communication messages (message-based framework) and communication processes (process-based framework) that address these challenges (Dutta 2011); and according to Edgar Schein, good communication happens through relationships (Schein 2016; Schein 2013; Schein 2009).

Communicative processes help build contexts for people to learn from one another as well as to co-create new ways of working together toward a social change mission (Dutta 2011). Additionally, socially innovative ideas can diffuse through communication channels of social capital, thereby contributing to non-profit agility as social change organizations consistently negotiate the changing needs of their stakeholders (Krlev, Anheier, and Mildenberger 2019). Communication in the non-profit sector can be challenging when multiple social networks interact with one another through diverse viewpoints (Lewis 2005). The literature draws attention to the pragmatic communication challenges faced by non-profits (Eisenberg and Eschenfelder 2009) as well as the need for non-profit research to focus more on communication as a process for co-creation and not solely a mode for information sharing (Koschmann et al. 2015). Further, since non-profit organizations tackle complex social problems, which often require collaboration across diverse stakeholders to diffuse innovation and accomplish change (Fisher et al. 2018), the change agent's use of good communication becomes vital to leading change in the non-profit sector (Rogers 2003). As a result, it is critical to learn more about the change agent's role in leading change (Kotter 1996; Conner 1999; Colville and Murphy 2006; Higgs and Rowland 2010) using communicative processes that bring people together to learn and act toward a common purpose (Seyranian 2014).

Affirming the broader communication challenges that exist within the diverse intersection of social systems that characterize the non-profit sector, Everett M. Rogers writes, "the structure of a social system can facilitate or impede the diffusion of innovations" (2003, 25). By this, he argues that the existing patterns of social relationships within a system constitute the social structure of that system, and thereby influence the flow of communication as well as the adoption of new ideas (Rogers 2003). Adoption of innovation is moderated by such factors as the strength of cultural norms, the power of social influencers, and the degree of heterogeneity within a social system (Assenova 2018; Sáenz-Royo, Gracia-Lázaro, and Moreno 2015; Rogers 2003). For every change agent, the challenge then becomes identifying and communicating to those outside of one's own dominant social systems of influence who may be the very people most in need of help or change (Rogers 2003). According to Rogers (2003), this challenge can exist because change agents are more effective at communicating with those who are most similar to them, especially in socioeconomic status. As a result, leading a change initiative that facilitates relationships across differences can be a difficult undertaking for change agents—especially with marginalized people groups who are oftentimes culturally and socioeconomically different than the leaders of the change institutions themselves.

Due to these challenges, focusing on communication messages and processes is essential because "change agents provide a communication link between a resource system with some kind of expertise and a client system" (Rogers 2003, 368) that may not be familiar with a change process or even may feel threatened by change itself (By 2005; Isern and Pung 2007; McKay, Kuntz, and Naswall 2013). Therefore, "communication may be a key mechanism of influence" for change agents (Seyranian 2014, 468) who desire to inspire, engage, and motivate different people to work together toward a social change mission. With this in mind, the questions that undergird the research in this book explored the "what" and "how" behind the relational communication strategies of change agents in non-profit organizations, which I talk more about in Chapters 3 and onward.

Notes

1 This model states that social change is distinguished by the following attributes: (1) it is aimed at creating change; (2) it addresses the root causes of social problems; (3) it is collaborative; and (4) it is not simple (Komives, Wagner, and Associates 2017, 235–236).
2 This resource was found in Roeger et al. (2012). Also, not all 501 (c)(3) organizations are included in this list because not all organizations, such as churches, need to apply for recognition of exemption unless so desired.
3 For descriptive definitions of these terms, refer to Helmut K. Anheier's book Nonprofit Organizations: Theory, Management, Policy. 2014. New York, NY: Routledge.

References

Anderson, Marc H. and Sun, Peter Y.T. 2017. "Reviewing Leadership Styles: Overlaps and the Need for a New 'Full-Range' Theory." *International Journal of Management Reviews* 19: 76–96.

Anheier, Helmut K. 2014. *Nonprofit Organizations: Theory, Management, Policy.* New York, NY: Routledge.

Anheier, Helmut K., Krlev, Gorgi, and Mildenberger, Georg. 2019. *Social Innovation: Comparative Perspectives.* New York, NY: Routledge.

Assenova, V.A. 2018. "Modeling the Diffusion of Complex Innovations as a Process of Opinion Formation through Social Networks." *PLoS ONE* 13, no. 5: 1–18.

Berzin, Stephanie Cosner and Camarena, Humberto. 2018. *Innovation from Within.* New York, NY: Oxford University Press.

Brothers, John and Sherman, Anne. 2012. *Building Nonprofit Capacity: A Guide to Managing Change Through Organizational Lifecycles.* San Francisco, CA: Jossey-Bass.

By, R.T. 2005. "Organisational Change Management: A Critical Review." *Journal of Change Management* 5, no. 4: 369–380.

Colville, I.D. and Murphy, A.J. 2006. "Leadership as the Enabler of Strategizing and Organizing." *Long Range Planning* 39: 663–677.

Conner, D. 1999. *Leading at the Edge of Chaos.* New York, NY: Wiley.

Dargie, C. 1998. "The Role of Public Sector Chief Executives." *Public Administration* 76: 161–177.

Drucker, Peter F. 1990. *Managing the Nonprofit Organization.* New York, NY: HarperCollins Publishers.

Dutta, Mohan J. 2011. *Communicating Social Change*. New York, NY: Routledge.

Eisenberg, E. and Eschenfelder, B. 2009. "In the Public Interest: Communication in Nonprofit Organizations." In *Handbook of Applied Communication*, edited by L.R. Frey & K.N. Cissna, 355–379. New York: Routledge.

Fisher, J.R.B., Montambault, J., Burford, K.P., Gopalakrishna, T., Masuda, Y.J., Reddy, S.M.W., et al. 2018. "Knowledge Diffusion within a Large Conservation Organization and Beyond." *PLoS ONE* 13, no. 3: 1–24.

Fry, Ron. 2021. "Lessons from the Field: The Emergence of Positive Institutions in VUCA Times." Advances in AI Workshop: 2021 AI Certificate Program. Weatherhead School of Management, Case Western Reserve University.

Gill, Stephen J. 2010. *Developing a Learning Culture in Nonprofit Organizations*. Thousand Oaks, CA: Sage.

Hassan, Z. 2014. *The Social Labs Revolution: A New Approach to Solving Our Most Complex Challenges*. San Francisco, CA: Berrett-Koehler.

Hecht, Ben. 2020. "Moving Beyond Diversity Toward Racial Equity." *Harvard Business Review*. Harvard Business Publishing. Accessed online January 2021.

Hersted, Lone and Gergen, Kenneth J. 2013. *Relational Leading: Practices for Dialogically Based Collaboration*. Chagrin Falls, OH: Taos Institute Publications.

Higgs, Malcolm and Rowland, Deborah. 2010. "Emperors with Clothes On: The Role of Self-Awareness in Developing Effective Change Leadership." *Journal of Change Management* 10, no. 4: 369–385.

Hill, Linda A., Brandeau, Greg, Truelove, Emily, and Lineback, Kent. 2014. *Collective Genius*. Boston, MA: Harvard Business School Publishing.

Hinrichs, Gina and Richardson, Cheryl B. 2015. *Large Scale Change for Non-Profits: A Playbook for Social Sector Capacity Building*. Charlotte, NC: Information Age Publishing, Inc.

Isern, J. and Pung, C. 2007. "Harnessing Energy to Drive Organizational Change." *McKinsey Quarterly* 1: 1–4.

Kania, John and Kramer, Mark. 2011. "Collective Impact." *Stanford Social Innovation Review*. www.ssireview.org

Kanter, R.M. and Summers, D.V. 1987. "Doing Well While Doing Good: Dilemmas for Performance Measurements in Nonprofit Organizations and the Need for a Multiple-Constituency Approach." In *The Nonprofit Sector: A Research Handbook*, edited by W.W. Powell. New Haven, 154. CT: Yale University Press.

Komives, Susan R., Wagner, Wendy, and Associates. 2017. *Leadership for a Better World*. San Francisco, CA: John Wiley & Sons.

Koschmann, M.A., Isbell, M.G., and Sanders, M.L. 2015. "Connecting Nonprofit and Communication Scholarship: A Review of Key Issues and a Meta-Theoretical Framework for Future Research." *Review of Communication* 15: 1–21.

Kotter, J. 1996. *Leading Change*. Cambridge, MA: Harvard Business School Press.

Light, P.C. 1998. *Sustaining Innovation: Creating Nonprofit and Government Organizations that Innovate Naturally*. San Francisco: Jossey-Bass Publishers.

Lewis, Laurie K., Hamel, Stephanie A., and Richardson, Brian K. 2001. "Communicating Change to 253 Nonprofit Stakeholders: Models and Predictors of Implementors' Approaches." *Management Communication Quarterly* 15, no. 5: 5–41.

Lewis, L. 2005. "The Civil Society Sector: A Review of Critical Issues and Research Agenda for Organizational Communication Scholars." *Management Communication Quarterly* 19: 238–267.

McDonald, R.E. 2007. "An Investigation of Innovation in Nonprofit Organizations: The Role of Organizational Mission." *Nonprofit and Voluntary Quarterly* 36: 256–281.

McKay, Kali, Kuntz, Joanna R.C., and Naswall, Katharina. 2013. "The Effect of Affective Commitment, Communication and Participation on Resistance to Change: The Role of Change Readiness." *New Zealand Journal of Psychology* 42, no. 1: 55–66.

Mirvis, Philip. 2017. "Redesigning Business to Serve Society: Joining Organization Development and Social Innovation." *OD Practitioner* 49, no. 3: 30–38.

Ospina, Sonia and Foldy, Erica. 2010. "Building Bridges from the Margins: The Work of Leadership in Social Change Organizations." *The Leadership Quarterly* 21: 292–307.

Ott, Steven J. and Dicke, Lisa A. 2016. *The Nonprofit Sector*. Boulder, CO: Westview Press.

Phipps, Kelly A. and Burbach, Mark E. 2010. "Strategic Leadership in the Nonprofit Sector: Opportunities for Research." *Journal of Behavioral and Applied Management* 11, no. 2: 137–154.

Roeger, K.L., Blackwood, A.S., and Pettijohn, S.L. 2012. *The Nonprofit Almanac 2012*. Washington, DC: The Urban Institute Press.

Rogers, Everett M. 2003 *Diffusion of Innovations (5th edition)*. New York, NY: Free Press.

Sáenz-Royo, C., Gracia-Lázaro, C., and Moreno, Y. 2015. "The Role of the Organization Structure in the Diffusion of Innovations." *PLoS ONE* 10, no. 5: 1–13.

Salamon, Lester M., Sokolowski, Wojciech, Haddock, Megan A., Tice, Helen S. 2013. *The State of Global Civil Society and Volunteering: Latest Findings from the Implementation of the UN Nonprofit Handbook*. Working Paper No. 49. Baltimore: Johns Hopkins Center for Civil Society Studies.

Schein, Edgar H. 2009. *Helping: How to Offer, Give, and Receive Help*. San Francisco, CA: Berrett-Koehler Publishers, Inc.

Schein, Edgar H. 2013. *Humble Inquiry: The Gentle Art of Asking Instead of Telling*. Oakland, CA: Berrett-Koehler Publishers, Inc.

Schein, Edgar H. 2016. *Organizational Culture and Leadership*. 5th ed. Hoboken, NJ: John Wiley & Sons, Inc.

Seyranian, Viviane. 2014. "Social Identity Framing Communication Strategies for Mobilizing Social Change." *The Leadership Quarterly* 25: 468–486.

Shier, M.L. and Graham, J.R. 2013. "Identifying Social Service Needs of Muslims Living in a Post 9/11 Era: The Role of Community-Based Organizations." *Advances in Social Work* 14, no. 2: 379–394.

Shier, M.L. and Handy, F. 2015. "From Advocacy to Social Innovation: A Typology of Social Change Efforts by Nonprofits." *International Society for Third-Sector Research* 26: 2581–2603.

Shier, M.L., McDougle, L.M., and Handy, F. 2014. "Nonprofits and the Promotion of Civic Engagement: A Conceptual Framework for Understanding the 'Civic Footprint' of Nonprofits Within Local Communities." *The Canadian Journal of Nonprofit and Social Economy Research* 5, no. 1: 57–75.

Spicer, A. 2020. "Organizational Culture and COVID-19." *Journal Of Management Studies* 57, no. 8: 1737–1740. 10.1111/joms.12625

Stroh, David Peter. 2015. *Systems Thinking for Social Change*. White River Junction, VT: Chelsea Green Publishing.

Taliento, L. and Silverman, L. 2005. "A Corporate Executive's Short Guide to Leading Nonprofits." *Strategy & Leadership* 33: 5–10.

Volf, Miroslav. 1996. *Exclusion and Embrace: A Theological Exploration of Identity, Otherness, and Reconciliation*. Nashville, TN: Abingdon Press.

Weerawardena, Jay, McDonald, Robert E., and Mort, Gillian Sullivan. 2010. "Sustainability of Nonprofit Organizations: An Empirical Investigation." *Journal of World Business* 45: 346–356.

Chapter 2

Setting the Table: A Conversation with Change Scholars

A story tends to exist behind every act of change. Many of those stories tell us information about the who, what, where, when, and why of change. Stories are a powerful means through which we explain our lives that include our trials and triumphs with change itself. Storytelling helps us connect what seems like separate strands of experiences into one coherent and meaningful narrative. Having grown up in a collective culture where the dinner table was just as much about sharing stories as it was about eating the food, I often experienced transformative moments while listening, learning, and interacting with whoever was present at the dinner table. Turns out that when it comes to changing the values, mindsets, and goals of an organization, the stories we tell around our organizational dinner tables have and will continue to shape organizational culture. For these reasons, I like to say that strategy is a story well told.

This chapter is a strategic storyline where I set the table of foundational scholarly work on the topic of leading change that supports the scope of my research and rolls out the red carpet for the practical implications of research findings. This means that when I talk about "the literature," I am asking you to imagine past scholars as friends sitting around the dinner table interacting with one another's stories—stories that can help us make meaningful connections to how we can better lead change in the present and future. As you read the literature review, I invite you to participate in the conversation. By understanding the existing literature on change as a story that's been told and written thus far, we can become wiser change agents who are more aware of the tables we set and lead change for greater human flourishing.

In the following pages, I review the precedent literature that builds the foundation of non-profit social change work on the intersection of research that integrates the topics of communication and relationships. The concept of change is complex. As a result, experts from various disciplines have offered explanations for change and its implementation (Lewis 2019). While this provides multiple perspectives on change that benefit its study and practice, "important insights into implementation and

DOI: 10.4324/9781003272243-3

important components of change are often isolated within disciplines or sub-disciplines" (Lewis 2019, 3). Therefore, it was necessary to take an interdisciplinary approach to crafting the precedent literature for this study. Overall, the precedent literature carries several general foci.

The first focal point in the literature recognizes non-profits as change agents in society (Norris 2019). In addition, Souder (2016) states that communication is one of the greatest challenges for non-profit social change agents as they work with a diverse set of stakeholders to accomplish their mission. Cnaan and Vinokur-Kaplan (2015) help us understand the concept of social change and its challenges as operationalized through the lens of social innovation, which intersects frequently with the literature on social change.

The second focal point considers the literature on social entrepreneurship and intrapreneurship as a way to holistically understand change agent work. The literature mentions that social entrepreneurs are considered change agents who innovatively solve society's problems (Brouard and Larivet 2010; Anheier 2014). Some researchers note that there is an awareness of serial entrepreneurship where social entrepreneurs move from one idea or innovation to the next (Sarasvathy, Menon, and Kuechle 2013; Berzin and Camarena 2018), and that research on intrapreneurship, especially the intrapreneur's ability to manage and sustain innovation, can add complementary value to our understanding of the complex work of change agents (Berzin and Pitt-Catsouphes 2015; Berzin and Camarena 2018).

The third focal point in the literature focuses on organization development's (OD) attention toward dialogic relationships to advance change, which is very relevant to the concept of social change itself as well as to the social entrepreneur who consistently navigates interpersonal dynamics. Bushe and Marshak (2015) state that dialogue is a way of conversing and relating with others that helps organizations like those found in the non-profit sector negotiate challenges that require the capacity to pivot and adapt. Researchers note that dialogue is an effective aspect of change (Brown and Duguid 1991; Crossan, Lane, and White 1999; Senge 2006; Tsoukas 2005) because its reflective nature can lead to more innovation. In addition, the literature reveals that the inclusive nature of dialogue provides a communicative platform for those who are socially marginalized (Dutta 2008a; Dutta 2011; Goldsmith and Burke 2011), thereby creating possibilities for social change by disrupting the accepted norms of conversational patterns.

Although communication is a shared experience with others (Ruben and Gigliotti 2016), it still requires our attention so that we address communicative practices that maintain division or marginalization (Dutta 2011). Specifically, communication that involves social change requires intentional reflection upon ways to create communicative processes that are truly inclusive and purposeful to include diverse voices (Dutta 2011).

Further, dialogue creates opportunities for collaboration with others, influencing collective impact through partnerships and social networks (Komives, Wagner and Associates 2017; Boyea-Robinson 2016).

The fourth focal point in the literature highlights collaborative social networks. Social networks for the purpose of collaboration characterize the non-profit sector's bent toward developing partnerships that can influence collective impact (Anheier, Krlev, and Mildenberger 2019). Collaborative social networks require frequent communication (Linden 2010) and have potential to generate innovative ideas by remaining adaptable over time (Plastrik, Taylor, and Cleveland 2014). Gittell (2016) uses the language of relational coordination to capture the essence of collaborative social networks as hubs that can change normative patterns of relating to others. Disrupting patterns of relationships as well as creating systems and structures to support new relational patterns describes the core of what non-profit social change organizations seek to do.

The fifth focal point in the literature integrates social learning and social change. This integration is important to the work of non-profit social change agents because of their tendency to work in collaboration with others, which requires people to learn new ways of relating and working together to accomplish shared goals. A wide spectrum of researchers and theorists such as Bronfenbrenner (1979); Heifetz, Grashow, and Linsky (2009); Dewey (1930); Mezirow (1996); and Fisher-Yoshida, Geller, and Schapiro (2009) recognize that learning happens through our experiences and relationships with others. When people learn in relationship with others, collective wisdom can emerge that can provide multi-dimensionality to a social problem (Briskin et al. 2009), thereby leading to positive outcomes in both oneself and others (Yang 2008). Due to the constant shifts in society, non-profit change agents manage social learning systems in continuous learning and capacity building (Gill 2010; Hinrichs and Richardson 2015).

In sum, the main theoretical frameworks on which this book rests include communication theory, relationship theory, educational theories of transformative and social learning, change theory, research in social innovation, and literature surrounding social entrepreneurship and intrapreneurship. These strands of literature provide a robust interdisciplinary framework that deepens our understanding of how non-profit change agents use relational communication strategies in their work.

Social Entrepreneurship and Intrapreneurship

The literature recognizes that social entrepreneurship has a variety of definitions (Tracey and Phillips 2007; Brouard and Larivet 2010; Anheier 2014; Rawhouser, Cummings, and Newbert 2019). For example, social entrepreneurs have been defined as "individuals who develop economically sustainable solutions to social problems" (Tracey and Phillips 2007, 264); or as "individuals who with their entrepreneurial spirit and personality will act as change agents and leaders to tackle social problems by recognizing new opportunities and finding innovative solutions" (Brouard and Larivet 2010, 45); or in reference to "innovation and initiation of social change in all areas of need" (Anheier 2014). When combined, social entrepreneurs seek to create social value by simultaneously stimulating social change and meeting social needs (Anheier 2014). In fact, Schwartz writes, "there is more agreement and overlap than discrepancy around the notion that these people cause disruption while repositioning systems to better support equity and create significant social change" (2012, 7).

Social entrepreneurs who "love to look at problems and build solutions" and who "do not set down roots in one area or venture" are known as "serial entrepreneurs" (Berzin and Camarena 2018, 15). Typically, they have "founder's attributes" but may lack "skill sets and know-how necessary to sustain a non-profit" (Berzin and Camarena 2018, 15). In the corporate world, when social entrepreneurs are found inside organizations, they are known as the "corporate social intrapreneur" (Mirvis 2017; McGaw and Malinsky 2020). The corporate social intrapreneur works to develop solutions to social problems by applying the principles of social entrepreneurship toward the work that happens inside the organization as a way to bridge alignment with the work that happens on the outside (Mirvis 2017). However, Thompson argues that "the main world of the social entrepreneur is the voluntary [non-profit] sector" (2002, 413). The non-profit sector also recognizes that its leaders possess a blend of skills often described of both social entrepreneurs and intrapreneurs (Berzin and Camarena 2018). Berzin and Camarena (2018) define intrapreneurship thus: "Intrapreneurship leverages not only the founder mentality of people within an organization who can develop an idea, but also the management skill sets needed to grow and sustain it" (15). A comprehensive approach to social innovation might consider the simultaneous need for social entrepreneurship and intrapreneurship (Berzin and Pitt-Catsouphes 2015). Given such realities, the non-profit sector is ripe for further research in social entrepreneurship, intrapreneurship, and innovation (Weerawardena and Mort 2012).

Although social intrapreneurship and entrepreneurship are primarily characterized by innovation, the process required for innovation can benefit from change processes used in organizational development, and vice versa (Mirvis 2017). For example, the concept of systems thinking that is familiar to OD leaders (Senge 2006; Mirvis 2017) has also been adopted by social entrepreneurs to think through innovative social change initiatives (Stroh 2015; Mirvis 2017). In addition, an area that has potential for greater mutually beneficial overlap includes the field of interpersonal communication (Mirvis 2017), which this chapter attempts to bridge by integrating dialogic practice and the creation of social change. OD leaders have focused attention toward developing tools for interpersonal communication and building relationships with others through the use of dialogic practice as a way to advance change (Busche 2013; Bushe and Marshak 2015; Mirvis 2017; Hastings, Schwarz 2021). These change tools can be helpful to social entrepreneurs who place importance on understanding the perspectives of the communities within which they seek social innovation (Schwartz 2012; Mirvis 2017). Given this brief description of OD approaches to change, as well as the characteristics of the social entrepreneur and intrapreneur, it is possible to imagine how the integration of these fields can create opportunities for change agents to innovatively tackle complex social change issues while simultaneously allowing the day-to-day operations of the non-profit itself to continue through dialogic OD (Drucker 1990, 12–13).

Dialogic Change and Dialogic OD

Dialogue is a process of communicating with and relating to others that helps us deal with the kind of adaptive challenges often found in the non-profit sector (Bushe and Marshak 2015, xiii). Dialogue encourages people to come together as equals to think, reflect, and create as a collective whole. It is "a conversation with a center, not sides" (Isaacs 1999, 19). Authors of dialogue write that the word "dialogue" comes from the Greek words dia (through) and logos (word or meaning) (Isaacs 1999, 19). Dialogic conversations are characterized by "streams of meaning" with and between and through people that "flow" to create shared meaning among a diverse group (Bohm 1996, 7). Paolo Freire writes that dialogue cannot exist without love, humility, faith, hope, and critical thinking (Freire 2000, 89–92). As such, there is a specific posture and attitude that is required for successful dialogue to take place. It is through dialogue that people come to gain a bigger picture of reality in ways that allow human beings to find significance and meaning in their collective capacity for transformation (Freire 2000, 88, 108; Vaughan 2011).

Numerous writers have explored dialogue as an effective aspect of change (Brown and Duguid 1991; Crossan, Lane, and White 1999; Senge 2006, Tsoukas 2005). For example, Senge writes about dialogue in the context of organizational teams learning to see one another and work together in new ways that sustain deeper systems changes (Senge 2006). Brown and Duguid argue that organizations that are "reflectively structured" tend to be more innovative and better able to handle potential gaps in the system (1991). Crossan, Lane, and White highlight different levels of learning that can take place in an organization and place the process of dialogue within the "interpretive" and "integrating" levels where the construction of new shared meaning through language and conversations can lead to "institutionalizing" through consistent repetition and solidification of new patterns of relating (1999). In his article, Tsoukas delineates at least three ways we understand organizational change (behaviorally, cognitively, and discursively), and argues that language matters in collective change efforts (2005).

In the world of OD, the literature distinguishes between "diagnostic OD" and "dialogic OD" (Bushe and Marshak 2009; Beckhard 1969; Bushe and Marshak 2015; Hastings, Schwarz 2021), which require either a diagnostic mindset where the focus of change is on changing people's behavior and what people do or a dialogic mindset where the emphasis is on changing mindsets and how people think (Bushe and Marshak 2015, 14). More specifically, the dialogic mindset is undergirded by the following key premises identified by Bushe and Marshak: (1) people socially construct reality and relationships; (2) people and organizations are meaning-making systems; (3) language influences the meaning-making process as well as change processes; (4) change is the result of changing conversations; (5) people need to interact with one another to surface differentiation on the journey toward coherence; (6) organizations and groups of people are in constant motions of change and therefore are "emergent"; (7) transformational change is emergent and cannot be planned; and (8) consultants are immersed within the organization and join the change process (2015, 17–18).

Transforming organizations through dialogic processes can be a difficult feat, especially when a dialogic mindset is not fully present (Bushe and Marshak 2015, 20). Since dialogic processes seek to bridge gaps in human thinking, acting, and being on a collective scale, dialogic OD recognizes three ways in which transformation is more likely to occur. First, a disruption needs to occur in an organization's current social order, meaning-making processes, and self-organizing patterns (Bushe and Marshak 2015, 20–21). Disruption creates pockets for new desired patterns of communication to emerge. The ability to initiate and sustain these new patterns creates the capacity for organizational change (Hedman and Gesch-Karamanlidis 2015). Second, since dialogic OD assumes that people socially construct reality through the use of language in the form of stories, new narratives need to be created and embraced by the collective, including those in positions of authority and power (Bushe and Marshak 2015, 22–23). When individuals interpret or reinterpret what they are experiencing, they begin to create new shared meaning that can change one's understanding and future actions (Crossan, Lane, and White 1999, 528). However, it is continued conversation, shared meaning by members of a group, and shared action over time that influence collective change (Crossan, Lane, and White 1999, 528; Seely-Brown and Duguid 1991). Third, new ideas and alternative ways of thinking, behaving, and relating need to be generated in order for transformation to occur (Bushe and Marshak 2015, 23). For example, when people learn to coordinate through a dialogic context, a space is created that is rich for deep transformation (McNamee and Moscheta 2015).

As such, change can come from anywhere in the organization—not just through a hierarchical, top-down approach. Some scholars argue that due to some people's perceptions that engaging in genuine dialogue is risky (due to loss of face, wanting to be polite, etc.), the presence of already existing webs of relationships creates the feeling of safety that is needed for authentic dialogue and innovation to happen (Albrecht and Hall 1991). In other words, whom one knows in an organization matters not only to how one engages in sharing information, but also regarding what one learns (Borgatti and Cross 2003). It is relational competency that needs to be cultivated in order to sustain dialogue and the possibilities of change over time (Bokeno and Gantt 2000). In fact, Bokeno and Gantt write,

> It is the relationships—rather than the learning labs, dialogue experiences, and training programs—that cultivate learning, disseminate learning, and maintain learning processes as a way of organizational life. (2000, 245)

Tsoukas argues that it is the "modality of relational engagement," or, in other words, the attitude that you tacitly convey to others regarding the kind of relationship you want to have, that makes dialogue productive (2009, 5).

According to Edgar Schein, successful dialogue requires an attitude of genuine interest and curiosity through the humble act of asking questions rather than telling people what to do (Schein 2013, 19). A humble attitude and a spirit of inquiry creates an atmosphere of psychological safety where people can begin to trust one another and build relationships (Schein 2016, 27–30). Varying depths of relationships form depending on the level of trust that is present (Schein 2016, 30–43)—a difference that is critical to the kinds of dialogue that emerge as well as the depth of transformation that is possible.

Dialogue, Social Change, and Collective Impact

The inclusive, relational nature of dialogue can provide a communications platform, space, processes, and resources to those who are socially marginalized (Dutta 2008a; Dutta 2011; Goldsmith and Burke 2011). Human conversation can cultivate the conditions for change in multiple spheres (Wheatley 2009). Talking with one another and discovering shared concerns or passions can restore hope that influences change on personal, collective, and societal levels (Wheatley 2009). Through conversation, human beings find courage to act as we begin to think together and learn from each other's experiences. In fact, Paulo Freire writes, "we cannot be truly human apart from communication ... to impede communication is to reduce people to the status of things" (1970, 123). By discovering more of our own humanity through communication with others, human beings learn how to transform the world together while simultaneously experiencing transformation within ourselves (Wheatley 2009).

The words we use to communicate with one another can influence generations of social systems and set in motion the creation of new cultures (Pearce 2007). W. Barnett Pearce recognizes communication's power when he writes, "The pattern of communication in which we handle our differences, more than the positions we take on the issues, or who wins the arguments, will shape the evolution of our social worlds" (Pearce 2007, 216). Traditionally, communication has often been perceived as a process in which information is transmitted from a sender to a receiver who listens, translates, and acts on the information received (Mcquail 2013; Ruben and Gigliotti 2016). However, alternative views of communication have recognized its complexity that involves interpretation based on cues, values, relational history, past experience, culture, context, previous learning, styles, physical and emotional abilities and disabilities, present life circumstances, and other factors (Ruben and Gigliotti 2016). Communication is a shared experience among human beings regardless of social identity (Ruben and Gigliotti 2016). This awareness can be helpful to organizations that desire to influence social change or work toward the public good.

However, communication can break down easily during the interpretation process between individuals due to the complexity involved in the construction of meaning, which often does not result in shared meaning (Watzlawick, Beavin, and Jackson 1967; Ruben and Gigliotti 2016). Sometimes, the complexity that is present within one individual does not align well with the complexity of another (Ruben 2016; Ruben and Stewart 2016). Therefore, when the gap in this mismatch is great, it is unlikely that a communicated message will be received in the exchange (Ruben 2016; Ruben and Stewart 2016). Everett Rogers recognized this mismatch through his research revealing that change agents were more successful diffusing innovation when interacting in relationships of homophily (the degree to which people who interact with each other are similar; examples include occupation, education, and other social identity factors) rather than heterophily (the degree to which people who interact with each other differ) (2003). For those who aspire to influence social change through collaborative relationships in our increasingly diverse world, communicative skill becomes an important means through which transformation occurs (Ruben and Gigliotti 2016).

As a result of the predicted growth in racial and ethnic diversity (Vespa, Armstrong, and Medina 2018), change agents may bear increased responsibility to grow a greater awareness of the degrees of difference between people and can begin with the recognition of and intentional work toward a deeper understanding of "the other." This phrase will be defined as used by Miraslov Volf in his book *Exclusion and Embrace* where he states that "the other" emerges as an enemy or an inferior through our acts to "assimilate," "expulse," or "subjugate" someone else.[1] We do this while remaining indifferent to the person's unique value and belonging within the patterns of interdependence that include the "mutuality of giving and receiving," which leads to collective learning and growth (1996, 67). Moreover, sometimes the assumptions we make about "others" are not formed as a result of first-hand experience, but rather from second-hand information or, even more profoundly, from "what we have not been told" (Tatum 1997, 4). As such, language, particularly how it is or is not communicated and who is involved in the communication process, can contribute to creating, maintaining, or changing our relationships with "the other" (Dunn and Eble 2015). As such, the communicative processes that an organization uses hold power to spread values and messages, to set agendas for what is discussed, and to determine how the discussions will take place, whose voices are heard and whose voices are silenced (Dunn and Eble 2015). This communicative influence should be considered by institutions that have a social change mission due to the relational engagement required on all levels of a social system to both create and sustain change over time (Bouwen and Taillieu 2004).

Communicative practices in general can also contribute to maintaining division or even creating marginalization by excluding or silencing certain voices (Dutta 2011). Marginalized groups typically do not have platforms to articulate their voices in the same ways that more powerful, resource-rich groups do (Dutta 2008a, 2008b; Dutta 2009; Dutta 2011). This is evident in knowledge construction when particular narratives get erased through narrator misinterpretation, or through decisions that are made in choosing whose stories get shared in dominant epistemic structures (Dutta 2011). Moreover, one of the assumptions underlying dialogic participation is that all participants stand on equal ground. The use of dialogue in spaces of social change should take into account the fundamental inequalities that exist with regards to access to communication and even more so dialogic spaces (Dutta 2011). Since dialogue requires having resources to gain knowledge about dialogue and to learn certain dialogic skill sets, dialogue can also unintentionally continue to be used as a tool for domination and control without critical reflection around its processes and rules of engagement (Dutta 2011).

Through the presence of marginal voices in discursive spaces, structural inequalities become disrupted and social change begins to occur

(Dutta 2011). In other words, voices that have been excluded or even erased are brought into the change arena to engage with voices that have more privilege and power. When this happens, practitioners and organizational change agents continuously negotiate their own identities in the face of their dialogic interaction with "the other" that challenges the very foundation of mainstream knowledge as well as their own personal assumptions and worldviews (Nagda 2006; Dutta 2011; Wheatley, Christman, and Nicolas 2012). When the process of dialogue is convened well, and when dialogue participants, regardless of social status, intentionally work to apply the principles of relational engagement of dialogue, the combination of voices has potential to impact social change on the global scale (Dutta 2011). As such, social change communication utilizes communication as a way to change social systems. Specifically, social change communication attempts to transform structural inequalities so that marginalized voices can experience the fruit from projects of redistributive justice (Dutta 2011). Therefore, social change communication reframes social change as one that emerges through a more inclusive and purposeful way of conversing with and on behalf of other people.

Given this, when considering the use of dialogue in social change, it becomes necessary not only to think about creating an open and inclusive field for conversation, but also to process together and collectively act toward transforming the structural disparities that exist and emerge along the way (Dutta 2011). As such, dialogue around the history of social structures becomes an important consideration when bringing together individuals from different social groups (Wheatley, Christman, and Nicolas 2012). The dialogic process helps individuals recognize their unique role and contribution within the group, thereby inspiring the emergence of a collective power that can influence social change (Grodofsky and Soffer 2011; Wheatley, Christman, and Nicolas 2012). When convening dialogue for social change, it is important to keep in mind that marginalized groups may evaluate the success of a dialogic process based on outcomes of social action rather than solely on the relational value that underlies the dialogic paradigm (Wheatley, Christman, and Nicolas 2012).

Hence, collective impact becomes an important piece and hoped-for outcome of dialogue. With the recognition that no single individual can tackle complex social challenges in isolation, the use of dialogue creates space for any "other" to participate and give voice toward the co-creation of social change efforts that directly affect his or her life and community (Kuenkel 2016). Including "the other" in dialogue is not an act that is "given," but rather, the intentions behind the use of dialogue are driven by a humble learning posture that genuinely seeks to listen and respect the voices around the dialogue circle as equal contributors to the social change movement. This kind of inclusive collaboration recognizes that, although organizations may have good intentions to influence so-cial transformation, the people directly affected by the imagined social change are in fact the "context experts" who are needed in order to sustain social change efforts well into the future (Boyea-Robinson 2016; Kuenkel 2016).

Moreover, collaboration with cross-sector partners creates momentum for wider collective impact (Komives and Wagner 2017; Boyea-Robinson 2016). When cross-sector partners work toward a common agenda and shared identity, organizations can accomplish significant collective impact by engaging a variety of community conversations and sharing information or resources to widen and deepen the social change agenda (Boyea-Robinson 2016). As mentioned before, however, this requires people to learn to develop "our human capacity for outcome-oriented dialogue, effective collaboration, and future-oriented collective action across institutional or national boundaries" (Kuenkel 2016, 5). Collaborating across boundaries demands human beings and organiza-tions to resist the barriers of organizational structures and systems as well as our individualistic natures (at least in the United States) that seek to keep collaboration at bay (Linden 2010). The ability to think and see interconnections rather than only parts helps guide collectively impactful boundary-spanning collaboration.

Collaborative Social Networks

Boundary-spanning collaboration is important in the non-profit sector because non-profit change agents often seek collaboration and partner-ships with others and desire collective action (Anheier, Krlev, and Mildenberger 2019). Collaboration "can be difficult to do; for people it doesn't come naturally, and much of our work life inside organizations is more about coordination and cooperation than collaboration" (Plastrik et al. 2014, 57). In addition, many non-profits work in isolation and be-lieve that they must compete with other organizations for funding (Goldsmith 2010). However, Anheier et al. (2019) describe non-profit organizations as "non-profit 'hubs' [that] frequently invite partners to contribute and thereby act as a bridge into collaborative constellations" (277). In fact, Anheier et al. (2019) state that the non-profit organization's ability to create connections "deserves closer attention, in particular as regards to its specific function in social innovation processes" (277).

Non-profit leaders who collaborate well "communicate laterally, look for ways to share ideas, and form relationships well. They tend to be natural networkers, understanding that organizational success relies at least as much on horizontal as hierarchical relationships" (Linden 2010, 1). Plastrik, Taylor, and Cleveland (2014) argue that social networks are composed of "individuals or organizations that aim to solve a difficult problem in the society by working together, adapting over time, and generating a sustained flow of activities and impacts" (5). Plastrik et al. call these "generative social-impact networks" because "they are designed to be a platform for generating multiple, ongoing kinds of change, not just accomplishing a single outcome" (2014, 5). Generative social-impact networks address complex social problems that are often unpredictable, change over time, and last a long while (Plastrik et al. 2014, 27). Because of their very nature, complex social problems "require generative responses—learning, innovation, and adaptation over long periods of time" (Plastrik et al. 2014, 27) that generative social-impact networks provide. In fact, Linden argues that "the most significant challenges facing our society cannot be addressed by any one organization. They all require collaboration among many organizations" (2010, 9). Further, the Arbinger Institute states, "the biggest lever for change is a fundamental change in the way one sees and regards one's connections with and obligations to others" (2016, ix). This suggests that building collaborative relationships with others broadens the possibilities for social change.

The advantages of a social-impact network include the accessibility of human talent outside a single organization and the flexibility to arrange such talent in strategic ways; the ability to connect with far more people than one's immediate social network; and the ability to share information quickly and widely (Plastrik et al. 2014). For social networks to be successful, however, "a network's communication infrastructure is essential ... because it will enable or impede collaboration" (Plastrik et al. 2014, 58). Further, depth of trust facilitates the quality of the communication and information sharing that flows through the social network (Plastrik et al. 2014). Likewise, Komives et al. (2017) note that "process is critically important in a collaborative effort" (121). Specifically, communication is "extremely important in the collaborative process" (121). In fact, "personal communication and group communication skills are key to enacting leadership for social change and practicing socially responsible leadership" (Komives et al. 2017, 139).

Gittell uses the language of "relational coordination" to capture the important mutual influence of communication and relationships (2016, 4; Bolton, Logan, Gittell 2021). She writes, "Relational coordination is simply the patterns of communicating and relating through which workers integrate their tasks into a whole" (2016, 4–5). Thinking beyond the relational coordination that can exist internally within an organization, Gittell argues that "relational coproduction" happens "when we extend relationships of shared goals, shared knowledge, and mutual respect to include our customers" (2016, 6). Gittell further argues relational coordination needs the support of "relational leaders who understand and respect the complexity of the work that their employees carry out every day" (2016, 6). Considered all together, this relational model of organizational change, in its essence, is about "communicating and relating for the purpose of integrating our work" (Gittell 2016, 82). Creating change, then, begins with changing the patterns of relationships as well as redesigning organizational structures and systems to support and sustain new ways of relating.

Social Learning and Social Change

As the research above suggests, collaboration requires learning in relationship with others. Relationships provide the context and conduit for many of our life experiences. Human beings develop and change through interacting systems of relationships that are part of what Bronfenbrenner calls the "ecological environment" (Bronfenbrenner 1979, 3). By using the metaphor of Russian dolls, Bronfenbrenner posits that human beings are consistently surrounded by various "nests" of influence or "proximal processes" that shape a person's development (Bronfenbrenner 1979, 3; Bronfenbrenner 1995). The innermost nest of influence includes environments such as the home or school, with the outermost nest of influence possibly including society or even abstract factors (Bronfenbrenner 1979). His point is that a person's perception of his or her reality is based on his or her interaction with the ecological environment and its interwoven parts that continue to change as the person traverses on the "ecological journey" (Bronfenbrenner 1995, 640). He argues that there are systemic reasons for the current lack of growth in human development and the resultant chaos of interpersonal engagement.

Similarly, Heifetz, Grashow, and Linsky argue that people are systems that have been influenced by a variety of "forces" acting upon them (2009, 181). From their perspective, human beings are "constantly changing parts of a constantly evolving larger system" (Heifetz, Grashow, and Linsky 2009, 184–85). As such, human beings are "subsystems" within the larger organizations of which they are a part (Heifetz, Grashow, and Linsky 2009, 54). Further, the authors argue that we live in a time of great interdependence where the challenges that organizations face are no longer technical and easily solvable problems, but rather are "adaptive challenges" that require a deeper systemic change on both the human and organizational levels (Heifetz 2010, 73). They are "adaptive challenges" because the challenges surface a disconnect between what an organization says it values versus what an organization actually values (Heifetz, Grashow, and Linsky 2009, 26). Solutions to these kinds of challenges typically require people to change how they operate through learning, shifting authority, experimentation, and patience through the process as they learn to discern how to simultaneously engage their past and present situations toward progression and change (Heifetz 2010, 74–76).

It is clear that learning through life experiences involves social inter-action with others (Dewey 1930). John Dewey argues that although experience is essential to learning, not all experiences are equally educative (Dewey 1930). Depending on the quality of an experience, some experiences can be mis-educative, thereby either "arresting or distorting" the growth of an individual (Dewey 1930, 25). Dewey believed that man or woman is a social self and that human beings long for social inter-action and, in fact, are interdependent with their environment (Dewey 1930). Human beings experience transformation through their experiences and can contribute to the construction of meaning with and for one another in the process of education, especially as a means to guiding children to become better citizens (Dewey 1930). As such, Dewey affirms the dignity and creative process of human beings as well as the process of growth, contribution, and reflection upon quality experiences that are necessary for transformative learning.

Part of the development into adulthood is fine-tuning the ability to re-flect upon one's beliefs to ensure validity as we seek to make decisions that are informed and thoughtful. Transformative learning theory posits that human beings think and act from a habitual frame of reference built through experience (Merriam 2008, 5). One's interpretation of an ex-perience can be revised and re-constructed through reflection typically generated by "disorienting dilemmas" that drive people to wrestle with unchecked assumptions (Mezirow 1996, 163). If committed to the process of reflection, there is a possibility that human beings can experience a transformation in how they see others and the world (Taylor and Cranton 2012, 6). It is important to note that new learning is not only connected with reflection upon our past experiences; our present experiences also require new learning. In fact, Merriam writes, "Experience is thus a re-source and a stimulus for learning" (Merriam and Bierema 2014, 106). Further, transformative learning does not happen only in the cognitive realm, but rather, the process of transformative learning engages the whole being of the person, thereby leading to a potential transformation in being (Merriam and Bierema 2014, 112) and having ontological implications.

Leahy and Gilly refer to transformative learning that takes place in relationships as "collaborative transformative learning" (CTL) (Fisher-Yoshida, Geller, and Schapiro 2009, 24–25), or "collaborative inquiry" (CI) (Kasl and Yorks 2002a; Yorks and Kasl 2002a; Yorks and Kasl 2002b). These collaborations keep relationships at the center and require that "all participants care about the group's work" by being willing to struggle through difficult conversations and places of tension (Fisher-Yoshida, Geller, and Schapiro 2009, 36). CI has been used and deemed particularly helpful for "pursuing questions that are personally devel-opmental, socially controversial, or require social healing" (Kasl and Yorks 2010, 316). Research on CI has shown its effectiveness in influencing personal and social transformations (Reason 1994; Yorks and Kasl 2002a), and when stewarded well, helps to create a "liberating structure" (Kasl and Yorks 2010, 1; Bray et al. 2000; Fisher and Torbert 1995) or "collaborative social space" (Yorks, Neuman, Kowalski, and Kowalski 2007, 355). In essence, learning and the possibility for transformation both take place within relationships (Yorks and Kasl 2002a) and have the potential then to build the capacity for social change to emerge by shifting the status quo.

This capacity for change can emerge from the wisdom that is gained through learning that happens through relationships. Briskin et al. refer to this kind of learning as "collective wisdom" (2009, xiii). They write that "wisdom is a form of knowledge marked by our ability to discern the inner qualities and relationships of a situation" and when the words collective and wisdom are used together, it is like "binocular vision, in which both eyes are used at once … a way of seeing with added dimension and depth" (Briskin et al. 2009, 8–9). Collective wisdom matters because "real change comes from an awareness of our deep connectedness" (Briskin et al. 2009, 9).

Additionally, the concept of wisdom is also conceptualized as a process—"a special kind of real-life process that is achieved after a person cognitively makes an unusual integration, embodies his or her ideas through action, and hence brings forth positive effects to both self and others" (Yang 2008, 64). Scholars have sought to understand wisdom as a process expressed through leadership. For example, Walter (1993) spoke of wisdom as a process that resulted in positive outcomes when leaders integrated thought with action. Küpers (2007) argued that wisdom is a process of the personal integration of mind and emotions along with the resultant expression of behavior within a community, society, or cultural context. Wisdom as process is relevant to this review of non-profit leadership not only because it informs interpersonal dynamics between leaders and followers, but also because, as researchers note, this kind of leadership is mirrored by non-profit leaders (Allen, Winston, Tatone, and Crowson 2018).

Social learning systems characterize the non-profit sector. Non-profit organizations have multi-stakeholder expectations that require relational investment and negotiation (Drucker 1990) influenced by constantly shifting social systems, increased competition, and complex regulations, just to name a few (Collins 2005; Gill 2010; Hinrichs and Richardson 2015). As such, social entrepreneurs and intrapreneurs who seek social change are encouraged to partake in a continuous process of learning and capacity building (Gill 2010; Hinrichs and Richardson 2015). Continuous learning and capacity building in turn build potential for systemic change, which is captured by Chris Blackmore (2010), who writes, "social learning is concerned in different ways with managing or influencing systemic change" (xi). In support, Gregory Batewson (1972) said, "The word 'learning' undoubtedly denotes change of some kind" (283). In practice, social learning takes place when (1) there is a "convergence of goals, criteria and knowledge leading to more accurate mutual expectations and the building of relational capital"; (2) there is "co-creation of knowledge, which provides insight into the causes of, and the means required to transform a situation"; or (3) there is a "change of behaviors and actions resulting from understanding something through action ('knowing') and leading to concerted action" (Ison 2010, 73–84).

Although the idea of learning in non-profits from a program-focused critique perspective is not new, sustaining transformative change needs a culture of learning (Gill 2010). A culture of learning is characterized by "an environment that supports and encourages the collective discovery, sharing, and application of knowledge" and is "continually growing, adapting, and becoming stronger" (Gill 2010, 5). Gill notes four levels of learning that occur simultaneously in non-profits (individuals, teams, whole organization, and community)[2] and refers to community level learning as the level that is externally focused and "one of the primary ways in which non-profits are different from other types of organizations" (Gill 2010, 34).

The interaction of these four levels of learning allows non-profit organizations to simultaneously improve their own organizations as well as the quality of life of the communities in which they envision social change. Moreover, the interdependent nature of non-profit work demands leaders who can convene a diverse representation of community stakeholders so that learning can begin to take place (Gill 2010). Further, a learning culture also needs leaders who can manage the complexity of diverse feedback and reflection that results when different perspectives interact in the same space (Gill 2010). This kind of collective collaboration involves the continuous development of relational networks, which would provide the trustworthiness needed for non-profits to build capacity at multiple levels (Gill 2010; Ott and Dicke 2016). As such, leaders of social change institutions can help reveal important new ways to approach challenging and messy problems (Ospina and Foldy 2010). Conversations and relationships that generate learning are a strong starting point for the co-construction of the future (Hinrichs and Richardson 2015).

Conclusion

The non-profit sector drives social change and innovation through interpersonal processes that bring people together to accomplish common goals. Characterized by multi-stakeholder involvement, the non-profit sector interacts with the very human need for relationships by building social capital through various communicative acts. Through dialogue and other forms of communication, social learning can take place. Collaborative learning has potential to create and sustain social change through collective impact as people create shared meaning together. Specifically, the non-profit sector can provide insight into how social change and innovation can take place through the confluence of relationships and communication. As such, there is an opportunity to understand the convergence of communication and relationships as strategies that would be helpful for leaders of non-profit social change organizations who seek to learn and collaborate with diverse stakeholders, including socially marginalized groups. This book contributes to the need for greater understanding by gleaning wisdom from non-profit change agents who developed trusting relationships through communication in order to collaborate with others toward a social change mission. The next chapters reveal how they navigated diverse relationships and the key themes that emerged from their work of leading change.

Notes

1 The entire quote by Volf reads: "Exclusion can entail cutting of the bonds that connect, taking oneself out of the pattern of interdependence and place oneself in a position of sovereign independence. The other then emerges either as an enemy that must be pushed away from the self and driven out of its space or as a nonentity—a superfluous being—that can be disregarded and abandoned. Second, exclusion can entail erasure of separation, not recognizing the other as someone who in his or her otherness belongs to the pattern of interdependence. The other then emerges as an inferior being who must either be assimilated by being made like the self or be subjugated to the self. Exclusion takes place when the violence of expulsion, assimilation, or subjugation and the indifference of abandonment replace the dynamics of taking in and keeping out as well as the mutuality of giving and receiving" (67).
2 For descriptions of these four levels of learning in non-profits, refer to Developing a Learning Culture in Nonprofit Organizations by Stephen J. Gill (2010).

References

Albrecht, Terrance L. and Hall, Bradford J. 1991. "Facilitating Talk about New Ideas: The Role of Personal Relationships in Organizational Innovation." *Communication Monographs* 58, no. 3: 273–288.

Allen, Stuart, Winston, Bruce E., Tatone, Gia R., and Crowson, Howard M. 2018. "Exploring a Model of Servant Leadership, Empowerment, and Commitment in Nonprofit Organizations." *Nonprofit Management and Leadership* 29: 123–140.

Anheier, Helmut K. 2014. *Nonprofit Organizations: Theory, Management, Policy*. New York, NY: Routledge.

Anheier, Helmut K., Krlev, Gorgi, and Mildenberger, Georg. 2019. *Social Innovation: Comparative Perspectives*. New York, NY: Routledge.

Arbinger Institute. 2016. *The Outward Mindset*. Oakland, CA: Berrett-Koehler Publishers, Inc.

Batewson, Gregory. 1972. *Steps to an Ecology of Mind*. New York, NY: Ballantine Books.

Beckhard, Richard. 1969. *Organization Development*. Reading, MA: Addison-Wesley.

Berzin, Stephanie and Pitt-Catsouphes, Marcie. 2015. "Social Innovation from the Inside: Considering the 'Intrapreneurship' Path." *National Association of Social Workers* 60, no. 4: 360–362.

Berzin, Stephanie Cosner and Camarena, Humberto. 2018. *Innovation from Within*. New York, NY: Oxford University Press.

Blackmore, Chris, ed. 2010. *Social Learning Systems and Communities of Practice*. United Kingdom: Springer London.

Bohm, David. 1996. *On Dialogue*. New York: NY: Routledge.

Bokeno, R. Michael and Gantt, Vernon W. 2000. "Dialogic Mentoring: Core Relationships for Organizational Learning." *Management Communication Quarterly* 14, no. 2: 237–270.

Bolton, Rendelle, Logan, Caroline, and Gittell, Jody Hoffer. 2021. "Revisiting Relational Coordination: A Systemtic Review." *The Journal of Applied Behavioral Science* 57, no. 3: 290–322.

Borgatti, Stephen P. and Cross, Rob. 2003. "A Relational View of Information Seeking and Learning in Social Networks." *Management Science* 49, no. 4: 432–445.

Bouwen, Rene and Tailieu, Tharsi. 2004. "Multi-Party Collaboration as Social Learning for Interdependence: Developing Relational Knowing for Sustainable Natural Resource Management." *Journal of Community and Applied Social Psychology* 14: 137–153.

Boyea-Robinson, Tynesia. 2016. *Just Change*. Charleston, SC: Advantage.

Bray, J., Lee, J., Smith, L.L., and Yorks, L. 2000. *Collaborative Inquiry in Practice: Action, Reflection, and Making Meaning*. Thousand Oaks, CA: Sage Publications.

Briskin, Alan, Erickson, Sheryl, Ott, John, and Callanan, Tom. 2009. *The Power of Collective Wisdom*. San Francisco, CA: Berrett-Koehler Publishers.

Bronfenbrenner, U. 1972. *Influences on Human Development*. Hinsdale, Illinois: Dryden Press.

Bronfenbrenner, Urie. 1979. *The Ecology of Human Development*. Cambridge, MA: Harvard University Press.

Bronfenbrenner, U. 1995. "Developmental Ecology through Space and Time: A Future Perspective. In *Examining Lives in Context: Perspectives on the Ecology of Human Development*, edited by P. Moen, G.H. Elder, Jr., and K. Lüscher, pp. 619–647. American Psychological Association. 10.1037/10176-018

Brouard, F. and Larivet, S. 2010. "Essay of Clarifications and Definitions of the Related Concepts of Social Enterprise, Social Entrepreneur, and Social Entrepreneurship." In: *Handbook of Research on Social Entrepreneurship*, edited by A. Fayolle and H. Matlay, pp. 29–56. Northampton: Edward Elgar Publishing.

Brown, John Seely and Duguid, Paul. 1991. "Organizational Learning and Communities Of-Practice: Toward a Unified View of Working, Learning and Innovation." *Organization Science* 2, no. 1: 40–57.

Bushe, Gervase R. and Marshak, Robert J. 2009. "Revisioning Organization Development: Diagnostic and Dialogic Premises and Patterns of Practice." *Journal of Applied Behavioral Science* 45, no. 3: 348–368.

Busche, Gervase. R. 2013. "Dialogic OD: A Theory of Practice." *OD Practitioner* 45, no. 1: 10–16.

Bushe, Gervase R. and Marshak, Robert J., eds. 2015. *Dialogic Organization Development: The Theory and Practice of Transformational Change.* Oakland CA: Berrett-Koehler Publishers, Inc.

Cnaan, R.A. and Vinokur-Kaplan, D. 2015. "Social Innovation: Definitions, Clarifications, and a New Model." In *Cases in Innovative Nonprofits: Organizations That Make a Difference* edited by R.A. Cnaan and D. Vinokur-Kaplan, pp. 1–16. Thousand Oaks, CA: Sage Publications.

Collins, Jim. 2005. *Good to Great and the Social Sectors.* Boulder, CO: Jim Collins.

Crossan, Mary M., Lane, Henery V., and White, Roderick E. 1999. "An Organizational Learning Framework: From Intuition to Institution." *The Academy of Management Review* 24, no. 3: 522–537.

Dewey, John. 1930. *Experience and Education.* New York, NY: Touchstone.

Drucker, Peter F. 1990. *Managing the Nonprofit Organization.* New York, NY: HarperCollins Publishers.

Dunn, Carolyn and Eble, Michelle. 2015. "Giving Voice to the Silenced: Using Critical Discourse Analysis to Inform Crisis Communication Theory." *Journal of Business Ethics* 132: 717–735.

Dutta, Mohan J. 2008a. "Participatory Communication in Entertainment Education: A Critical Analysis." *Communication for Development and Social Change: A Global Journal* 2: 53–72.

Dutta, Mohan J. 2008b. *Communicating Health: A Culture-Centered Approach.* Cambridge: Polity.

Dutta, Mohan J. 2009. "Theorizing Resistance: Applying Gayatri Chakravorty Spivak in Public Relations." In *Social Theory on Public Relations*, edited by O. Ihlen, B. van Ruler, and M. Fredriksson, pp. 278–300. London: Routledge.

Dutta, Mohan J. 2011. *Communicating Social Change.* New York, NY: Routledge.

Fisher, D. and Torbert, W.R. 1995. *Personal and Organizational Transformations: The True Challenge of Continual Quality Improvement.* London: McGraw-Hill.

Fisher-Yoshida, Beth, Geller, Kathy Dee, and Schapiro, Steven A. 2009. *Innovations in Transformative Learning: Space, Culture and the Arts.* New York, NY: Peter Lang Publishing.

Freire, Paolo. 1976a. *Pedagogy of the Oppressed.* New York, NY: Continuum.

Freire, Paolo. 2000. *Pedagogy of the Oppressed.* New York, NY: Continuum.

Gill, Stephen J. 2010. *Developing a Learning Culture in Nonprofit Organizations.* Thousand Oaks, CA: Sage.

Gittell, J.H. 2016. *Transforming Relationships for High Performance.* Stanford University Press.

Goldsmith, Stephen 2010. *The Power of Social Innovation.* San Francisco, CA: Jossey-Bass.

Goldsmith, Stephen and Burke, Tim Glynn. 2011. "Ignore Citizens and Invite Failure." *National Civic League*. John Wiley & Sons: 14–18. 10.1002/ncr.20043

Grodofsky, M.M. and Soffer, G. 2011. "The Group as a Community Social Agent: The Case of the Bedouin." *Social Work with Groups* 34, no. 2: 190–202.

Hastings, Bradley J. and Schwarz, Gavin M. 2021. "Leading Change Processes for Success: A Dynamic Application of Diagnostic and Dialogic Organization Development." *The Journal of Applied Behavioral Science* 58, no. 1: 120–128.

Hedman, Eerika and Gesch-Karamanlidis, Eleni. 2015. "Facilitating Conversations that Matter Using Coordinated Management of Meaning Theory." *OD Practitioner* 47, no. 2: 41–45.

Heifetz, Ronald, Grashow, Alexander and Linsky, Marty. 2009. *The Practice of Adaptive Leadership*. Boston, MA: Harvard Business Press.

Heifetz, Ronald. 2010. "Adaptive Work." *The Journal Kansas Leadership Center*. 72–77.

Hinrichs, Gina and Richardson, Cheryl B. 2015. *Large Scale Change for Non-Profits: A Playbook for Social Sector Capacity Building*. Charlotte, NC: Information Age Publishing, Inc.

Isaacs, William. 1999. *Dialogue and the Art of Thinking Together*. New York, NY: Random House Inc.

Ison, Ray. 2010. "Traditions of Understanding: Language, Dialogue and Experience." In *Learning Systems and Communities of Practice*, edited by C. Blackmore, pp. 73–88. United Kingdom: Springer London.

Kasl, E. and Yorks, L. 2002a. "Collaborative Inquiry for Adult Learning." *New Directions for Adult and Continuing Education* 94(Summer): 3–11.

Kasl, E. and Yorks, L. 2010. "Whose Inquiry Is This Anyway? Money, Power, Reports, and Collaborative Inquiry." *Adult Education Quarterly* 60, no. 4: 315–338.

Komives, Susan R., Wagner, Wendy, and Associates. 2017. *Leadership for a Better World*. San Francisco, CA: John Wiley & Sons.

Kuenkel, Petra. 2016. *The Art of Leading Collectively: Co-Creating a Sustainable, Socially Just Future*. White River Junction, VT: Chelsea Green Publishing.

Küpers, W.M. 2007. "Phenomenology and Integral Phenol-Practice of Wisdom in Leadership and Organization." *Social Epistemology* 21: 169–193.

Lewis, Laurie. 2019. *Organizational Change: Creating Change through Strategic Communication*. Hoboken, NJ: Wiley.

Linden, Russell M. 2010. *Leading across Boundaries: Creating Collaborative Agencies in a Networked World*. San Francisco, CA: Jossey-Bass.

McGaw, Nancy and Malinsky, Eli. 2020. "Unlocking the Potential of Corporate Social Intrapreneurship." *The Aspen Institute and the Fetzer Institute*. 1–40.

McNamee, Sheila and Moscheta, Murilo. 2015. "Relational Intelligence and Collaborative Learning." *New Directions for Teaching and Learning* 143: 25–40.

Mcquail, Denis. 2013. "Reflections on Paradigm Change in Communications Theory and Research." *International Journal of Communication* 7: 216–229.

Merriam, Sharan B. Ed. 2008. *Third Update on Adult Learning Theory*. San Francisco, CA: Jossey-Bass.

Merriam, Sharan B. and Bierema, Laura L. 2014. *Adult Learning: Linking Theory and Practice*. San Francisco, CA: Jossey-Bass.

Mezirow, J. 1996. "Contemporary Paradigms of Learning." *Adult Education Quarterly* 46: 158–172.

Mirvis, Philip. 2017. "Redesigning Business to Serve Society: Joining Organization Development and Social Innovation." *OD Practitioner* 49, no. 3: 30–38.

Nagda, B.A. 2006. "Breaking Barriers, Crossing Borders, Building Bridges: Communication Processes in Intergroup Dialogues." *Journal of Social Issues* 62, no. 3: 553–576.

Norris, Kendall. 2019. "Collective Impact: How Nonprofits Can (and Should) Serve as Catalysts for Transformative Social Change." *USBE & Information Technology* 72: 72–76.

Ospina, Sonia and Foldy, Erica. 2010. "Building Bridges from the Margins: The Work of Leadership in Social Change Organizations." *The Leadership Quarterly* 21: 292–307.

Ott, Steven J. and Dicke, Lisa A. 2016. *The Nonprofit Sector*. Boulder, CO: Westview Press.

Pearce, W. Barnett. 2007. *Making Social Worlds: A Communication Perspective*. Malden, MA: Blackwell Publishing.

Plastrik, Peter, Taylor, Madeleine, and Cleveland, John. 2014. *Connecting to Change the World*. Washington, DC: Island Press.

Rawhouser, Hans, Cummings, Michael, and Newbert, Scott L. 2019. "Social Impact Measurement: Current Approaches and Future Directions for Social Entrepreneurship Research." *Entrepreneurship Theory and Practice* 43, no. 1: 82–115.

Reason, P. (Ed.). 1994. *Participation in Human Inquiry*. Thousand Oaks, CA: Sage.

Rogers, Everett M. 2003. *Diffusion of Innovations* (5th edition). New York, NY: Free Press.

Ruben, B.D. 2016. "Communication Theory and Health Communication Practice: The More Things Change, The More They Stay the Same." *Health Communication* 31: 1–11.

Ruben, Brent D. and Gigliotti, Ralph A. 2016. "Leadership as Social Influence: An Expanded View of Leadership Communication Theory and Practice." *Journal of Leadership and Organizational Studies* 23, no. 4: 467–479.

Ruben, B.D. and Stewart, L. 2016. *Communication and Human Behavior* (6th ed.). Dubuque, IA: Kendall Hunt.

Sarasvathy, Saras D., Menon, Anil R., and Kuechle, Graciela. 2013. "Failing Firms and Successful Entrepreneurs: Serial Entrepreneurship as a Temporal Portfolio." *Small Business Economy* 40: 417–434.

Schein, Edgar H. 2013. *Humble Inquiry: The Gentle Art of Asking Instead of Telling*. Oakland, CA: Berrett-Koehler Publishers, Inc.

Schein, Edgar H. 2016. *Organizational Culture and Leadership*. 5th ed. Hoboken, NJ: John Wiley & Sons, Inc.

Schwartz, Beverly. 2012. *Rippling: How Social Entrepreneurs Spread Innovation throughout the World*. San Francisco, CA: Jossey-Bass.

Seely-Brown, I. and Duguid, P. 1991. "Organizational Learning and Communities of Practice: Toward a Unified View of Working, Learning and Innovation." *Organization Science* 2: 40–57.

Senge, Peter M. 2006. *The Fifth Discipline: The Art and Practice of the Learning Organization.* New York, NY: Doubleday.

Souder, Lawrence. 2016. "A Review of Research on Nonprofit Communications from Mission Statements to Annual Reports." *International Society for Third-Sector Research* 27: 2709–2733.

Stroh, David Peter. 2015. *Systems Thinking for Social Change.* White River Junction, VT: Chelsea Green Publishing.

Tatum, Beverly Daniel. 1997. *Why Are All the Black Kids Sitting Together in the Cafeteria?* New York, NY: Basic Books.

Taylor, Edward W. and Cranton, Patricia. 2012. *The Handbook of Transformative Learning: Theory, Research, and Practice.* San Francisco, CA: Jossey-Bass.

Thompson, Janice L. 2002. "The World of the Social Entrepreneur." *International Journal of Public Sector Management* 15, no. 5: 412–431.

Tracey, P. and Phillips, N. 2007. "The Distinctive Challenge of Educating Social Entrepreneurs: A Postscript and Rejoinder to the Special Issue on Entrepreneurship Education." *Academy of Management Learning and Education* 6, no. 2: 264–271.

Tsoukas, Haridimos. 2005. "Afterword: Why Language Matters in the Analysis of Organizational Change." *Journal of Organizational Change Management* 18, no.1: 96–104.

Tsoukas, Haridimos. 2009. "A Dialogical Approach to the Creation of New Knowledge in Organizations." *Organization Science* 20, no. 6: 1–17.

Vaughan, C. 2011. "Dialogue, Critical Consciousness and Praxis." In *The Social Psychology of Communication*, edited by D. Hook, B. Franks, and M.W. Bauer, pp. 46–66. Basingstoke, England: Palgrave Macmillan.

Vespa, Jonathan, Armstrong, David M., and Medina, Lauren. 2018. "Demographic Turning Points for the United States: Population Projections for 2020 to 2060." *U.S. Department of Commerce.* www.census.gov

Volf, Miroslav. 1996. *Exclusion and Embrace: A Theological Exploration of Identity, Otherness, and Reconciliation.* Nashville, TN: Abingdon Press.

Walter, G.A. 1993. "Wisdom's Critical Requirement for Scientific Objectivity in Organizational Behavior Research: Explicit Reporting of Research Values." In *Handbook of Organizational Behavior*, edited by R.T. Golembiewski, pp. 491–524. New York: M. Dekker.

Watzlawick, P., Beavin, J., and Jackson, D. 1967. *Pragmatics of Human Communication: A Study of Interactional Patterns, Pathologies, and Paradoxes.* New York, NY: Norton.

Weerawardena, Jay and Mort, Gillian Sullivan. 2012. "Competitive Strategy in Socially Entrepreneurial Nonprofit Organizations: Innovation and Differentiation." *American Marketing Association* 31, no. 1: 91–101.

Wheatley, Margaret J. 2009. *Turning to One Another: Simple Conversations to Restore Hope to the Future.* San Francisco, CA: Berrett-Koehler Publishers.

Wheatley, Anna, Christman, Seth T., and Nicolas, Guerda. 2012. "Walking the Talk: Reflections from a Community Focused Dialogue Series." *Journal for Social Action in Counseling and Psychology* 4, no. 1: 1–17.

Yang, Shih-ying. 2008. "A Process View of Wisdom." *Journal of Adult Development* 15: 62–75.

Yorks, L. and Kasl, E. 2002a. "Learning from Inquiries: Lessons for Using Collaborative Inquiry as an Adult Learning Strategy." *New Directions for Adult and Continuing Education* 94(Summer): 93–104.

Yorks, L. and Kasl, E. 2002b. "Toward a Theory and Practice for Whole Person Learning: Reconceptualizing Experience and the Role of Affect. *Adult Education Quarterly* 52(3): 176–192.

Yorks, L., Neuman, J., Kowalski, D., and Kowalski, R. 2007. "Lessons Learned from a 5 Year Project within the Department of Veterans Affairs: Applying Theories of Interpersonal Aggression and Organizational Justice to the Development and Maintenance of Collaborative Social Space." *Journal of Applied Behavioral Science* 43: 352–372.

Chapter 3

Discernment: A Change Leader's Superpower

As a change leader who values people, I have worked on crafting a people-centric values statement that acts as my north star in every interaction and consulting opportunity. On that statement includes leadership advice from one of my doctoral advisors, Dr. Donald Guthrie: "Listen to understand; speak to serve." Listening is the starting point of our change leadership. And listening happens beyond what our ears hear. In Korea, we have a term called *noonchi* (roughly translated as "eye force/power"—it's the art of discerning mood and context by "listening" with our eyes and reading the room). I try to practice embodied listening by activating my noonchi in order to discern the tacit dimension. What's your noonchi telling you? Listening to understand better, can help you serve your people better. This chapter captures the clear and strong call to lead change with and through discernment.

"There are a lot of things that are super strategic and super important; a lot of things that are really urgent. But I think there is important work, especially of a change leader, of discernment" (Non-profit Change Leader). This quote captures the critical work of discernment that is required of change agents. For the purposes of my research, I define discernment as:

> "Listening and responding" to others with the intent to "sift through our impulses, motives, and options to discover which ones lead us closer to love and compassion for ourselves and other people and which ones lead us further away" (adapted from Henri Nouwen's definition, 2013, xv).

Doing the work of discernment helps change agents see how and why people work together for positive social change.

The 26 non-profit change leaders in my research use discernment to influence successful social change through their relational communication strategies, as evidenced by their self-reporting and self-description. Descriptions of their own change success are in direct contrast to the

DOI: 10.4324/9781003272243-4

history of change implementation failure noted in the literature (Beer and Nohria 2000; Sirkin, Keenan, and Jackson 2005; Holbeche 2006). It is encouraging that the change leaders in my research give hope for change success. They also challenge us to consider discernment as part of the work of a change process that helps give guidance to managing change and the transitions that accompany it.

It is notable to mention that the practice of discernment was often developed through the very life experiences that influenced change leaders' desire to enter into the work of social change, which we talked about in Chapter 1. Change leaders in this study had experienced personal or societal challenges that motivated them to define reality, design a path forward, and do the hard work to get there. Practicing discernment helped change agents understand interrelationships between people and systems in order to lead change well. By seeking understanding of interrelationships, change agents also saw fragmentation in both relationships and social systems. Despite this, change agents worked diligently to discern their participation in the change they believed to be possible and already taking place in their midst. Change agents consistently had a relational lens that shaped their desire to work toward a new and better reality for others. With an others-centered focus, change agents approached social change with a committed carefulness to the act of discernment—without which change could easily be pushed forward without any consideration of restoring value and dignity to those who need the change most.

Further, their commitment to the practice of discernment was continuous throughout a change process. For this reason, I argue that their ability to discern is better described as a state of being. The act of discerning became a natural part of who they were as a result of the consistent exercise of discernment. Unlike habits, however, which can unconsciously take over our everyday lives, the practice of discernment as an automatic response to leading change was still intentional and grounded in the valuable insight gained to benefit the change agent's work. With an awareness that change is constantly happening around them, participants were also keenly aware that consistent change requires consistent learning in order to adapt. This in turn requires consistent discernment to know how to enter into, engage with, and exit out of a change process—a process that involves constant communication with a variety of stakeholders. Therefore, discerning change agents continuously learn how to navigate change in ways that communicate care and advocacy for others along the change process. Learning continuously gave wisdom toward the change process and also contributed to the internal heart change that often took place within the change agents themselves. This discerning learning posture gives change agents both credibility and trustworthiness to guide change initiatives that would bring value to organizations and society alike. As such, the uniqueness of discerning change agent leadership is key to change success.

It is important to note that while discernment was present throughout the participants' work toward a social change mission, and described as a primary value, discernment surfaced predominantly in figuring out how to catalyze urgency for change that would serve others well versus change that would cause harm. The root of their hope to serve others well did not come from a desire to please people. Rather, their hope was rooted in a passion to respect or restore dignity to people. This is a critical distinction that brings to the surface the motives of change agents in this study. More will be said about this in later chapters, but when people experience a change leader's genuine love and care they not only want change for themselves, but also want to be partners in moving the larger change mission forward. For now, let's review the prominent theme of discernment that emerged from this research.

Discerning the Change Landscape

Discerning the change landscape was a strong value and praxis among the majority of change leaders. They communicated that discerning the change landscape involved growing in self-awareness of their own change agency as well as in awareness of change that occurs on the interpersonal, community, and systemic levels so that participants could more strategically interact with different change processes. In order to understand the complexity of this theme, it is necessary to begin with an explanation of two common beliefs shared by the majority of change leaders in this study that contribute to the architecture for theme one.

Two Common Beliefs

Two common beliefs were shared across change leader responses: First, change is possible; Second, change is already in motion. Let's unpack what these mean.

Change Is Possible

All change leaders had strong conviction that change is possible. This conviction was seen in their commitment to the work of change in their respective contexts and to the people they serve. Change leaders stated that despite the challenges of encountering resistance to their change mission, or to an illusion of who they are as stereotyped by race or gender, the belief that change is possible gives them hope for a different and better reality. For example, one change leader mentioned that society is "frayed and broken, kind of like a cloth," but believes we can make it better by "reweaving the fabric" of society to "bring everything back together so it's harmonious." Moreover, this change leader reflected on her belief that change is possible by stating: "You shine the light where you are and then it draws others to do that. And that's really how the world changes. It's not a big grandiose thing." In addition, another change leader confidently proclaimed: "I would say that you absolutely can change the world" and encouraged us to be cautious of people who say we cannot change the world. He continued to share that he has "seen the positive impact" of his organization's work inspiring other leaders in his community to adopt similar change strategies used in his organization.

Further, a long-term commitment to the work of change has given change leaders opportunity to witness various pockets of change as a result of their efforts, which in turn, have ripple effects toward bigger change. In fact, one change leader shared her interpretation of bigger change, which "is the change you can't quantify" because for her, "it's how you change your heart as a change agent, how your team changes, and how people change in love and relationship and care and understanding of others." Similarly, another change leader expressed her belief that change is possible by sharing that even small acts of change can be powerful when the world "operates on the disproportionate impact of small things."

Change Is Already in Motion

All change leaders held the belief that change is already in motion. Change leaders did not hesitate to share their belief in the reality that change is always happening around us. Some mentioned that their organizations become part of the bigger change process taking place in the world as they seek to partner with others in change-making. As a result of participating with others in the bigger change process, many change leaders shared the understanding that change cannot be fully controlled. For example, one change leader said: "And change will happen regardless of what you do. It will be what it's going to be." Also, other change leaders stated: "Sometimes you follow the momentum or follow where God is working, where He wants you to work and recognize." Reflecting on the uncontrollable, yet beautiful nature of change, one change leader shared a "favorite moment" he had earlier this year when his organization decided to empty out its bank account in order to give money to a partner organization that was financially struggling. In awe that both organizations continued to thrive in their collaboration, he said: "Nothing stopped. I think that's the beauty of what we're trying to do. We can have not a penny to our name and nothing stops. We didn't even feel the emptying of our bank account." Similarly, another change leader noted that his work is "in alignment with God's purposes" of change that have been prepared in advance for him to step into.

Influenced by these two beliefs that change is possible and already in motion, change agents discern the change landscape as a means to carefully and strategically think through different approaches to change. Due to the frequent repetition of discernment as a data point, it is a theme that is divided into two subthemes: (1) discernment of self, and (2) discernment of contextually nuanced layers of change. It is important to note that change leaders spoke of discernment throughout a change process and not simply as one step in the beginning of a change process.

Sub-theme: Discernment of Self

Most change leaders spoke about the importance of having a discerned self-awareness that results from a foundational posture of humility. According to their stories, having a humble yet still confident posture is critical to understanding the reality of one's change agency as a leader and helps build integrity through more authentic interactions with others. Authentic interactions then strengthen social rapport and influence in spaces where change is most needed. For example, one change leader said: "I think you just have to be authentic, you know, you got to have a lot of humility. You got to be confident all at the same time." In order to illustrate the interaction of humility and confidence, he continued to share that he strategically meets with CEOs dressed casually in jeans and a collared shirt as a way to nonverbally communicate his desire for genuine relationship. The combination of humility and confidence is also seen in participant expressions of genuine curiosity in their communication with others. For example, another change leader said she values "soliciting input from community members themselves." A different change leader referenced the work of expressing genuine curiosity as "deep work." She said it requires "the deep work of knowing your audience; the deep work of knowing the issues; the deep work of knowing the challenges and environment; and the discernment of an invitation." Similarly, other change leaders continually desired to purposefully ask questions that strengthened relationships. Through the process of asking questions, change agents were able to discern the most impactful ways they could influence change in a particular context and with a particular group of people.

Through a foundation of humility, a change leader also stated, "You got to be willing to take smart risks and admit when you're wrong." Participants did not hesitate to share that making mistakes, admitting ignorance, or taking ownership of failures might be uncomfortable but is necessary to be a change agent. Again, having a measure of humility to admit mistakes, ignorance and failures did not negate the confidence and commitment to the change they were working toward. One change leader's story helps illustrate this:

You sometimes hear people use the phrase—"fake it until you make it." I think that is a terrible thing. When I'm sitting across, for example, from a chartered accountant in India, which is the equivalent to a lawyer here in the US who would set up businesses, there is no way in the world I can fake understanding international tax law for an Indian private limited company that's going to be owned by a US non-profit. I think it's much better to take a posture of learning and humility with conviction and commitment than it is to fake it until you make it.

In their willingness to be honest and vulnerable regarding their short-comings, change leaders stated that it is important to ask for help. One change leader expressed: "Being very open and honest about what our needs are and transparency, vulnerability, humility, knowing what you don't know and knowing where to get that help from." Also, another change leader said of himself and his wife (who co-founded the orga-nization): "We have just been committed to learn what we need to learn and have been willing to be the novice in the room and ask all the silly questions and be willing to be wrong in many ways. But then also to make sure that we're getting people on our team that are experts in their area." In congruence with the stories that have already been shared, yet another change leader said it is important to communicate when she does not have answers as well as to articulate what she can and cannot offer. During times when she does not know what to do for others, she said, it is critical for her to remain connected to these relationships as a learner.

Further, most participants reflected on the importance of having self-awareness of their strengths as well as their limitations, which helped them further discern the work of change in which they should or should not engage. For example, a change leader who founded his organization shared: "This year, we hired a CEO. I'm not a CEO, I was not born a CEO. I don't have the skills of a CEO. I don't have the experience of a CEO. And just because I founded the organization doesn't mean I should be the CEO. Now, you have to be ready to check your pride at the door. All I care about is solving this problem." Similarly, another change leader's growth in self-awareness of his own ethnic identity and cultural values, which act as both strengths and limitations, has raised the need to discern behavioral changes depending on context. He said:

We were taught a certain way—we were taught to respect our elders; we were taught to always listen to the voice of people; we were always taught to play second; to be in the background. And I've had to realize that those are the values I grew up with; those are not the same values that other cultures have. So, I stay true to who I am while recognizing that I might have to do things differently depending on the place I'm working out of.

Similarly, a different change leader expressed that while on staff at another organization, he became more aware of his strengths as a pioneer and entrepreneur rather than someone who maintains projects over long periods of time. Resonating with this experience, another change leader, who also learned about her entrepreneurial strengths while working as an artist, stated: "Artists don't learn a lot of technical or administration skills, and in fact, I'm not very good at those things. But I think being an artist has allowed me to create what I want to see in the world and I have to figure out how to make that actually become reality." Focusing on an experience with an international partner, yet another change leader told a story about a time when she realized the gift of recognizing her own limitations as influencing others' flourishing by leaving space for someone else to exercise their gifts. Specifically, she pointed to the importance of "recognizing where I end and where I begin; where my organization ends and where it begins."

In sum, change leaders reported that discernment of self begins with a posture of humility, which allows them to embrace the reality of their strengths and limitations as well as to authentically communicate mistakes and lack of knowledge. As such, change leaders felt that continuous growth in self-awareness was essential to effective change agency.

Sub-theme: Discernment of Contextually Nuanced Layers of Change

Many change leaders talked about the tri-fold work of change that happens in the interpersonal realm, in the community realm, or in the systemic realm. Often, their stories captured an intersection of these different layers of change that showcased the complexity of the change agent role in working toward change efforts in all three areas simultaneously. The acknowledgment of this intersection as well as the discernment of the different layers of change seemed critical to the development of change management and strategy.

Discerning the work of change in the interpersonal realm is directly connected to the kind of one-on-one relationships that change leaders developed in their respective contexts. One change leader's quote captured the interpersonal realm well when he said: "Change happens at the rate of relationships." Another change leader reflected on how his organization focused primarily on this layer of change during the early start-up years: "The interpersonal is like relationship building, you know, neighbor to neighbor." In the same story, he said that once his team got to know different people in the neighborhood, they were able to advocate for change based on the needs of their neighbors—needs they could no longer ignore due to their proximity to those same needs as well as the solidarity that was built through developed relationships. Another change leader also shared that knowing her neighbors intimately helped her "zoom out" from locating issues to the people or to the neighborhood to the larger issues that impact the way her neighbors live and move through the world. Specifically, she said:

> Speaking from my experience, that whole relationship building with my neighbor, listening to their story, having them care about me—it flipped all the concepts I had about "what am I really here to do?" And I think there were some interesting realities I learned around the goal of love and justice. That challenges me to see my role in a different way and expands my ideas of my own sense of comfort and my own sense of need as I'm learning and hearing about theirs. This is why I need to vote; I need to actually participate in local government. I don't like the trash always piling up on my block— that's an issue. Why is that happening? Those kinds of real things became ways I can now serve my neighbor because one, it bothers them, and two, it bothers me because I live here now too.

Similar to the relationship-building that takes place on the individual level, change leaders mentioned that discerning change on a community-wide level consists of building relationships with organizations within the community doing parallel social change work with the hopes of developing partnerships that can influence collective change. Change leaders stated that community partnerships are important because centering voices from the community can be a more effective way to influence change than leading with voices from people, some like the participants themselves, who do not have the same lived experience within the community in which they seek change or with the people they seek to serve. For example, one change leader said: "Most good community development comes from the ground up, not from outsiders." In addition, another change leader stated: "If communities want to hear what we have to say, hearing from one of their own is the most powerful and effective way to get that. That's really how community change happens."

Moreover, one change leader, who founded an organization that helps incubate other non-profit organizations across the Chicagoland area, remarked: "So many times I see people living in disenfranchised neighborhoods who are actually the most innovative people to come up with ideas to solve problems in their community than the outsiders who come in and try to take care of their needs." Speaking more specifically about the strategy of partnerships to influence community-wide change, another change leader said: "We partner with other existing organizations that have been here long term and have specific initiatives. They have holistic measures they're a part of. Our folks will come alongside them and partner with them in these community-wide efforts."

Last, change leaders shared that discerning the systemic layer of change is necessary yet complicated because of the need to figure out the historical narrative that lies beneath the intersection of problems within a specific context. Change leaders stated that the complexity of systemic change almost always requires partnerships with others in order to make progress. They also stated that these partnerships were more than creating collective change, but were also relationships that fed mutual courage, perseverance, and commitment over time. One change leader who helped give language for the different layers of change reflected that he cannot love his neighbor without advocating for change on a systems level. He said:

> If we're not changing the systems, what are we really changing because the systems have such a longer-term impact. We can't love our neighbors if we're not also advocating for change on a larger level. And systemic change—you can't do that as just an individual and you can't just do that as an organization. It has to be a very collaborative thing with not just local organizations but also national organizations that are addressing systemic issues.

Likewise, another change leader who made distinctions between different layers of change said: "And then the third one is a systems approach to change. If people aren't getting their checks from finance on time, you don't go yell at finance and say: You get these checks issued! Rather, you say: Where in the system is it broken that this person is not getting her check on time because other people are having the same problems. No band-aid approaches, but you really look at systems change."

In particular, change leaders talked frequently about discerning systems-level change through a more holistic understanding of contexts. According to change leaders, this discernment and understanding came through "research," which included a lot of listening and asking questions. Participants identified research as part of the process of relationship building, specifically as it relates to their intentionality in drawing out and gathering as much information as possible that would inform change-making decisions. They mentioned that taking the time to "conduct research" brought clarity to three areas: (1) to identifying the change agents already working in a particular context; (2) to the reality of a situation; and (3) to understanding another person's perspective. As such, "conducting research" added value to a change agent's ability to build social networks, to understand which processes of change would be most effective based on contextual cues, and to better discern the timing for communication strategies that would influence the movement of change. To this point, one change leader said that her organization uses research to "position [their] communications and strategically engage change" based on the information gathered from people in the community. Likewise, another change leader's words captured the importance of prioritizing contextual research well when she commented without hesitation that research is "where I would start" because if "you see something that needs to be changed then the first thing you need to do is your homework." She continued to say that "research is key" because "you don't want to reinvent something that's already going on, or maybe your view is not really what's going on. Maybe there's something else that's really happening or there's something deeper." Similarly, many change leaders mentioned that research requires being present and embedded within a community in order to understand the hopes and felt needs of people. One change leader shared that embeddedness is critical to developing trust so that people feel safe to communicate their hopes for change. For example, she stated that she does "a lot of listening to the community; interviewing focus groups, surveys, listening, listening, listening." She continued to share that research helps her develop a strategy for what to do next:

> Then we determine what we're going to do because the community knows what change they want to see. That's the work that has to happen and that I don't think can happen from a distance either. You need to be really embedded within the community because there has to be this element of trust that people are really going to tell you what they think. And in order to do that you have to be identified as part of the community, not as an outsider coming in.

Thus, gathering data resulted from being in relationship and in "small group meetings," or as one change leader liked to phrase it, from having "boots on the ground." Another change leader also remarked, "It's getting to know people, listening to what their felt needs are, what they want to see, what are their dreams, what are their hopes for the community, how can we support them and their dreams." One change leader commented that her organization uses design thinking to discern the perspective of others within a specific context:

> I think one of the great things is we approach most issues, challenges, all of those kinds of things with a design-thinking mindset. This means starting with empathy. What do our stakeholders, whoever they may be, need? What would they think about this? How can we figure it out from that perspective and then problem solve from there? I think when I see a need or an issue, I just step back and ask questions first.

Further, change leaders valued research because discerning the internal change agents within a particular context was key to change leaders who desired to come alongside others within the community who had already been doing the work of change for many years. When speaking of identifying internal change agents, participants often framed their remarks by sharing their desire to add value to a context rather than creating competition or even harm. One change leader talked passionately about his conviction to come alongside internal change agents. He suggested:

> What if we changed the paradigm to not just pursuing whatever we dream because we could fund it, but that we actually support the dreams of the leaders who are already here. They could do it better. They've been doing it longer. They just don't have the same access to funding. What if we supported them? How do I, as a person who comes from more privilege, who has had the wind at my back with support from a community, then say, "Well, I don't want to just pursue this for myself when other people don't have that same access." How do I leverage this to help other people have that same access to a job, to college, to start their non-profit or to keep it running and keep the doors open?

This value-add mentality was also important to other participants, like this change leader who said: "I want to be more valuable to you than you could potentially be to me. Now, does that always work out? No. But we approach it with that mentality." Similarly, another change leader stated: "We have to come in with some kind of added value that really will help them before we talk much about a collective vision." Finally, yet another change leader expressed: "So I would say in communities for which we are trying to be a good neighbor, or a good presence to, try to look for what is the hook—what is the pointer or the thing that God has already started to do in this community and then, is there a particular thing that we can be helpful in." Change leaders strongly shared a desire to add value to their respective contexts that would depend on how well they discerned the change that was already taking place and the internal change agents whom they sought to come alongside.

Although change leaders placed systems change as one of their top priorities, they did not hesitate to share the challenges that accompany it. Some change leaders mentioned nuanced challenges with systems change that resulted from context-specific problems. For example, some change leaders stated that contexts with a history of corruption made systems change especially difficult. In these cases, they said they approach systems change through a generational lens, seeking change in young people to become the new roots within a community. For example, one change leader who works in a historically corrupt city in the United States said: "So the change then has to deal with how do we change these systems?

How do we catch kids when they're still very, very young and impressionable, and keep them from gravitating to the corners?" Another change leader said:

> In terms of systems change, that is probably the most difficult in terms of working in one of the most corrupt countries in the world. Our strategy is raising up the youth. If we can impact 6,000 high school students next year; if we can educate the 21 survivors we have in our community, our hope is that they're going to become the next doctors and lawyers and social workers and people who are in high positions of authority in the country so that when they grow up and the older generation dies off, a new generation can come up that is more just, more equitable, more compassionate towards the poor.

In sum, change leaders communicated the importance of discerning change on the interpersonal, community, and systemic levels in order to be able to engage possibilities for change strategically. Moreover, because change leaders were fully aware of overlap between these three layers, they expressed that discernment of each separately was critical to know how and when to engage them simultaneously. Further, change leaders mentioned it was important to discern the contextual nuances that interacted with the different layers of change in order to best meet needs and collaboratively work with others.

References

Beer, M. and Nohria, N. 2000. "Cracking the Code of Change." *Harvard Business Review* 78, no. 3: 133–141.

Holbeche, L. 2006. *Understanding Change: Theory, Implementation and Success*. London: Butterworth-Heinemann.

Nouwen, Henri. 2013. *Discernment*. New York, NY: HarperOne.

Sirkin, H.L., Keenan, P., and Jackson, A. 2005. "The Hard Side of Change Management." *Harvard Business Review* 83, no. 10: 108–118.

Chapter 4

A People-Centric Approach to Catalyzing Urgency for Change

Catalyzing urgency for change requires wisdom and courage—two characteristics of change leaders that stood out as I listened to their stories. Wisdom to know *when* to catalyze urgency, and *how* to go about it with the right motivation. Courage to name *what* is urgent, and *why* it matters. If we think about it, it shouldn't be so hard to catalyze urgency for change in our fast-paced world. However, perhaps this is exactly why it's so hard. Leaders catalyze change without fully thinking through the immense burden people carry simply by living through our volatile, uncertain, complex, and ambiguous world. As a result, we experience change fatigue no one wants to address. But, here's the key phrase that begins every research question in this book—*in relationship with others.* When we prioritize our relationship with others in the change process, we begin to care about leading change with others who trust us and the process, who receive and lean in to the change we're trying to communicate, and who understand the change mission now and over again.

This chapter illumines findings from change leader responses to the first research question: "In relationship with others, how do non-profit change agents catalyze a sense of urgency for a desired change?" Change leaders were asked questions about their experiences regarding the work that takes place before change is introduced and how they advocate for change. Findings were originally organized under four main themes: (1) discern the change landscape; (2) develop relationships of love and trust; (3) disrupt the current narrative; (4) design the organization for change. However, given the importance of discernment, I've lifted that theme into its own chapter (Chapter 3). This chapter will provide insight into the three remaining themes re-organized as: Theme 1—Develop Relationships of Love and Trust; Theme 2—Disrupt the Current Narrative; and Theme 3—Design the Organization for Change.

Theme 1: Develop Relationships of Trust

All change leaders mentioned the need to build trust with people as part of the work that takes place before a change is introduced. Investing time

DOI: 10.4324/9781003272243-5

to develop relationships with others provided a strong foundation for catalyzing an urgency for change because people began to communicate their hopes and dreams for change once trust was built. In fact, one change leader said: "We will be able to progress at the speed of trust." One way change leaders built trust was through genuine curiosity to understand others. A change leader passionately explained that "communication has to start with getting to know each other" with emphasis placed on the other person. She said relationships should be built "not for the purpose of getting to a shared vision, but with a genuine belief that relationships are the foundation for everything. It's where you build trust." Another change leader reiterated that she advocates for change through trusted relationships. She stated: "I want to build trust and have a solid partnership. Then you could introduce change in those systems." Likewise, another change leader replied: "It took a lot of time to build relationships over time, and to just earn trust in the small things so that we can be trusted with the big things." One change leader beautifully articulated the essence of building trust with others as a strong foundation for catalyzing the urgency for change when she shared:

> The first thing that came to mind is trusting relationships and partnerships. Very rarely in my organization do we identify a change and then go, "Okay, these are the three or four different partners we need to then build relationships with before we introduce the change." There is a lot of relationship/partnership building that happens pre-change. Late last week, I was in a meeting with somebody and we usually grab coffee when she's in town. It could be ten coffees that she and I grab, but it does mean that on the dime we are able to quickly work together when change issues come up. So, I think there's a need to find people who share the same ethos, or same affinity, same world view, but maybe have complementary audiences, complementary strategies, and complementary levers. It's the deep building of those relationships so when change is introduced, you actually have something to stand on because negotiating things like, "Okay, how are we going to communicate with each other? What are the things that are non-negotiable for us?" You often don't have time for that stuff. When you introduce change, you introduce quite a lot of stress into the system. And those are often not the best environments in which to negotiate some of those tricky things.

Sometimes, the genuine desire to get to know someone was challenging for participants, but well worth the risk of investment rather than not trying to build relationships at all. One change leader named this challenge when he said: "Now that's not always easy because you're going to be vulnerable, right? Some people are going to abuse that. But for the most part I believe that people are good and the net will be way more positive than if you're always thinking about yourself." Similarly, another change leader mentioned: "When we get down to the level where we're ready to work with people, we're looking at things like values and trust and a lot of things that are not that tangible. It's like going with your intuition and thinking I could work with this person based on these conversations and then we pilot stuff and we see what happens." Every so often, challenge came in the form of critics or direct opponents. In response to critics, one change leader said that her organization sought ways to build trust over time by continuing to provide access to relationship building through communication. She shared:

> Yes, we have come across a lot of critics or people that didn't want to support. The way that we've gone about it is just to continue to be respectful and continue to have an open dialogue and open avenues for relationship with that individual. And in recognizing that for many of them, it may take a long time, maybe several years for us to prove ourselves and to earn their respect.

When racial dynamics prevented trust building, participants revealed that relationships with key members of the community brought down relational barriers and helped build trust. For example, a White change leader who works primarily in African–American communities stated: "Until there's trust established, nothing is going to happen. I never ever show up in all African–American meetings alone anymore. I bring one of my African–American colleagues. And, if there is a meeting that's going to be predominantly attended by White business people, my Black brother never shows up without me." This statement was shared in the context of how this particular change leader and his colleagues worked to target the reality of the racial biases they encountered. For them, specific relational connections and friendships broke down biases and helped shift perspectives so that trust could be built.

The second way change leaders built trust was through a commitment to the people they serve, the community in which they live, and to the work of change itself. Observed commitment over time was a critical factor for others to identify change leaders as part of the community, rather than simply an outsider with self-centered motivations for change. One change leader shed light on this type of trust building when she expressed the importance of being "embedded within the community because there has to be this element of trust that people are really going to tell you what they think. And in order to do that you have to be identified as part of the community, not as an outsider coming in." Another change leader passionately stressed the importance of commitment to building trust when she shared:

I think buy-in is generated after there's trust built that this is going to last. And we were really lucky to be able to do that on credit from the church that started before us. They had about ten years' presence in the community before our non-profit started. And in a lot of ways practically, because we shared their building, because we had a lot of personnel overlap, we were able to use a lot of that relational capital in a way that otherwise I think we wouldn't be where we are today without that, because of that trust and buy-in.

In addition, another change leader communicated that long-term commitment can influence different kinds of change to ultimately make a bigger impact: "We start with trust building and partnership, and some of it results in trying to fund things together. Some of it is just a long-term commitment to working together."

Change leaders often expressed that commitment to people, a context, or to the work of change itself involves sacrifice. One change leader said: "It's a sacrifice. You're going to have to grind, you're going to have to keep chopping wood, right?" Another change leader who highlighted the intersection of personal and community sacrifice stated: "You know, I think it comes at a personal sacrifice. It comes at a community sacrifice because there are times where you have to make decisions, you have to experiment and try things that people are not gonna agree with or they might not know where you're going." A change leader who works to save children's lives through providing clean water, identified similar challenges: "It's people's lives, right? You're talking about people drinking highly contaminated water and you're talking about children being afraid to go on the toilet that's going to collapse on them. It's the inspirational leaders that we work with who have given up so much in their lives to do what they are doing."

The third way change leaders built trust was by earning their change agent credibility through actions or metrics that supported their intentions. For example, one change leader stated:

I think if you're going to advocate for change, you also have to be extremely credible. I just can't stand in front of a CEO or CFO or a CMO and be unreasonable. I think that you have to be willing to be that in some way and do something transformative, say something transformative to get them thinking a little differently, but then you have to back it up with action and with results.

As mentioned previously, the act of listening was of chief value to change leaders. However, most change leaders said that listening was only the beginning of trust building, by also adding that acting upon the stories heard or the feedback received was just as critical to building deeper levels of trust with those they serve. One change leader captured this well in her reflection:

> I think what I've learned is that a lot of people who have been active historically are tired of lending their voice and not seeing anything happen. I think that community work and seeding the ground and getting feedback and buy-in and ownership ultimately is preeminently important. But it has to be paired with direct action or else you lose the trust you would have built, right? And you take three steps back.

Change leaders also mentioned that tracking and sharing metrics helped build their credibility and trustworthiness as change agents. It should be noted that when speaking of metrics, however, change leaders communicated that knowing the impact of their own work also affirmed their purpose. One change leader named it this way: "You have to be able to demonstrate the efficacy of what you're doing, otherwise you're just going through the motions. More than any donor, more than any volunteer, we have to know that what we're doing is working because we are dedicating our lives to this work. So why would we settle for something that's not working?" Also worth mentioning is that some change leaders expressed that although their organizations kept track of metrics, some of the most transformative and relational aspects of change were the most difficult to measure. For example, one change leader said: "I think a lot of the beauty of our work that is hard to measure is that we bring people together." Another change leader also shared that her organization uses metrics, but that some successes are harder to measure than others. She declared:

> Yeah, we have outcome measurements. We're trying to work on getting better metrics. But there's also a more nebulous thing that I remember from one of our annual benefits. We did a video of a story of this guy named Jeff who would stand in the corner and talk to himself all day long. He was mentally ill. He began to take meds so he could actually have a conversation with someone. I mean, that's an outcome. That's a success. Is he going to get his college degree? Probably never, but he's talking to people. There are different levels of success, but what we want to know is that people's quality of life is improving and that they're taking steps.

Overall, participants continuously voiced that when the people they serve could see their successes through action and change, trust was deepened. Deeper trust led to more opportunities to influence change. For example, a change leader said: "We stuck it through for the last ten years. And in the neighborhoods we've worked in, our crime is reduced by about 50 percent. And so, we're in a different place where now—there are neighborhoods that are pulling us to them; There are other cities saying we want your services."

Despite some challenges, developing relationships of trust was a critical part of the work that took place before change was introduced. Moreover, trust provided a launching ground to catalyze urgency for change and was deepened by a change agent's commitment over time as well as through action that built up the credibility of the change agent.

Theme 2: Disrupt the Current Narrative

Change leaders consistently shared they had to bridge differences as a way to disrupt the presently understood narrative of a community or people group with the hope of creating "a stronger collective social fabric." One change leader referred to these communicative acts of disruption as "radical candor." Many change leaders talked about disruption mainly through acts of communication and as part of their work that was critical to catalyzing an urgency for change. One change leader talked about how catalyzing an urgency for change required a consistent disruption of ideas spread through communication. He described communicative disruption this way: "Naturally, every space has its walls and ceilings. Can we build in capacity to kind of blow those walls and ceilings off and help reimagine [a new collective reality]?" Another change leader, who was very emotionally charged about the need for communicative acts of disruption, said: "Advocacy is also changing the narrative. It's telling a different story. It's trying to teach even folks that are outside of our communities about the issues that are happening inside our community."

Change leaders mentioned that disrupting the current narrative was uncomfortable, but also good and necessary so that deeper understanding and relationships could be built with others who are different from themselves and from one another. One change leader reflected on his non-profit change agent role and said: "I think you have to be willing to have uncomfortable conversations and do uncomfortable things." He continued to tell a story of when he had an uncomfortable conversation with someone by trying to disrupt this particular person's way of building a sustainability model that was more about self than other. He said: "This is what I mean by uncomfortable conversations where you're like, 'Okay, I really respect and love what you're doing. I appreciate your efforts. But the children we serve, they don't really care about your pride.'" In addition, another change leader shared a story about the uncomfortable exchange that takes place within oneself in the disruptive bridge-building work that she does between high-income, predominantly White neighborhoods and low-income, predominantly Black neighborhoods. She shared: "Isn't it good for me to feel that uncomfortableness? Yeah, it definitely is."

From change leaders' perspectives, bridging communities of people was disruptive because it required communicating and interacting with others across difference—acts that pushed people out of their own comfort zones of isolation into uncomfortable zones of community. One change leader captured this well through a story she shared of a time when she brought a wealthy donor together with a low-income student who was the direct recipient of funds. She stated:

> Oftentimes our funders also have a very limited scope of exposure to certain things. It could be argued that donors are very isolated as well. In some ways, it can be seen as: "Okay, here's the adult with the power and here's the student without the power," but actually in this conversation, they're both coming with strengths and areas of growth and when they have this conversation, they recognize those. So, if you're both isolated in this kind of way, and then you get to talk to each other, there's less of an isolation by bringing these communities that often don't get to be together; together in a meaningful way.

Further, change leaders mentioned that talking about the needs that exist in the world disrupted people's way of thinking and living, and therefore made them uncomfortable. Coupled with some causes that were "unpalatable" topics for the everyday dinner table, change leaders said that discomfort levels rose for some of them when trying to advocate for change around these more uncomfortable causes. However, change leaders continued to mention that building bridges between people together was still the preferred solution. One change leader highlighted this when he said:

> If we're really going to bring about change, then we have to talk about the needs that exist. Particularly with sex trafficking, because it's in many ways, kind of an uncomfortable, unpalatable topic. For some people, it feels so distant, so nameless, faceless, even though it happens in every country. So early on, one of the things that we chose to do is, we chose that we aren't going to really talk much about statistics. Instead, what we're going to do is try and bring the humanity back into something that's exceptionally inhumane and we're going to try and connect person to person.

Some change leaders specifically shared that they used different platforms, such as social media or protesting, as a way to disrupt the current narrative. One change leader said that her organization works "with organizers on the ground to help organize impacted communities and lift up their voices." She encourages her team to "definitely try and use media and communications as a key strategy." One Asian–American change leader emphasized that for him, sharing on social media was very disruptive given his own cultural background, where he was "always taught to be quiet, to get our work done." Now more comfortable in his own skin, he said: "Now I'm a lot more comfortable with myself. So, I'm willing to put more things out on social media and I'm willing to be out there and talk about things a little bit more to really share perspectives and thoughts. I'm a Christian at the end of the day. So, when you click my social media articles, in some way it's almost like I'm trying to insert my faith into some of the things that I'm doing there. I just hope that it sparks conversations." Another change leader, whose work involves protest disruption, shared this experience to illustrate her interpretation of disruptive communication:

> I head over to the Office of the Department of Border Protection where a group of us are calling for an end to family detentions and we're delivering a letter that's signed by about 8,000 women. I walk a couple blocks, get stopped by a presidential motorcade. So, they shut down the streets. Everyone has to stay on the sidewalk. There's about fifteen of us from that protest who just happened to get blocked there. The President waves at us from his limo. We're all carrying our signs: "Free the children! Free the children!"

Although participants shared that having disruptive, uncomfortable conversations were good and necessary, many participants voiced that sometimes they had to willingly endure personal emotional pain or risks to their reputation. However, it should be noted that participants expressed an overwhelming amount of positivity, courage, and tenacity in their awareness and acceptance of this reality as simply a part of their advocacy work. For example, one change leader shared what happened when she disrupted a system: "I know not everybody likes me right now. That's okay. It hurts my feelings, but I'm not gonna let it get to me. I ride it out. Then, call it what it is when it comes out—Yes, that was messy. But look what we learned." Similarly, another change leader noted: "Sometimes things are broken and you give lots of opportunity to change and lots of opportunity for input and you try different things. But sometimes as a leader, you have to step in and take charge and say, 'No, we're going to do it this way.' That's always a last resort and that's kind of dangerous to do, but sometimes you have to do that." Another change leader passionately remarked:

> If you hear something that doesn't jive, or you know to be untrue, or offensive, you cannot be afraid to let your voice be heard. But

actually, that's a hard lesson to learn, right? I mean some spaces you're in can be intimidating. I'm afraid of looking dumb, or saying the wrong thing. You can't be afraid to say things that you know to be right and true. You have to just speak your piece and not be afraid to advocate.

Overall, change leaders remarked that disrupting the current narrative was necessary as part of the process of bringing diverse groups of people together and worth the potential costs. Whether disruption took place on social media, through group interactions, or protests, change leaders said that discomfort was an expected and typical result of change agent work.

Theme 3: Design the Organization for Change

Change leaders placed strong emphasis on designing their organizations for change as a way to catalyze urgency for change. When they described different ways of designing their organizations for change, two sub-themes were repeated: First, strategic alignment toward a missional "North Star," or organizational values; and second, creating organizational systems and structures that facilitated change.

First, following the organization's North Star, or guiding values and principles, allowed non-profit change agents to catalyze an urgency for change. One change leader who talked about the process she takes when making decisions around organizational change stated: "We have the North Star, right? So, one, we always try to keep to the North Star. That's what we're always doing." Change leaders often interchanged the words "North Star" and "mission." A Christian change leader talked about how a deeper understanding of his organization's mission led to greater advocacy efforts. He said:

Our mission tag line is: "love God, love people, nothing else matters." That's been our organizational motto for twenty-one years, but there's been this development of understanding of our role too and unique responsibility toward the marginalized and to the oppressed. If Jesus says love your neighbor as you love yourself, that is a form of justice. That's equity. Make sure that your neighbors have access to the same things that you have access to; to have the same resources that you did. So, to be loving my neighbor is about pursuing justice.

Similarly, another change leader said that her organization sought rootedness in its core values, which gave their work integrity. For example, she mentioned: "We have set such clear core values of what always roots us back and those core values within themselves allow for fluidity too of how we approach change based on who's part of our community. And so, advocating for change has looked like me working around the word integrity. Do we have integrity to these core values in the work that we're doing?"

Being mindful of guiding principles helped change leaders advocate for change because the principles not only guided planned change, but also provided reasons behind why change was necessary. For example, one change leader shared: "I think a great way to be an advocate for change is to understand the why and plan for change. Planning for change is a great way to advocate for change because if you have a strong strategy in place and you've got a strong reason to change something, it makes your job as an advocate a lot easier." Other change leaders also talked about "strategic streams" being the guiding principles that shaped change initiatives. For example, one change leader said: "We can help catalyze a holistic movement in our area through strategic streams: unify, amplify, and multiply. We focus on each one of those three strategic streams."

Second, most change leaders proclaimed that designing their organizations for change involved creating systems and structures that facilitated change efforts. Change leaders had both intuitive and learned wisdom to set up their organizations as part of the work that needed to be done before change was introduced. Setting up organizations for change gave way to the development of communication channels, relationships, and other processes that were critical to catalyzing urgency for different types of change. One change leader described: "You have to set up your organization so that no matter what level you're at, you don't have fear in coming to your supervisor. We want to set it up so that we can say, 'Hey, you got an idea, please share it.' We don't want people to feel like they don't have a voice, so that's really important in all of the things that we do." Providing access for others to share their voice was also important to another change leader who said:

> I have been at this organization from the beginning and because of that I feel I have a lot of freedom and I have a lot of access to bring change. But, I have noticed that it's a different story for staff who are brand new and their avenues to access change are very different. I have to be cognizant that other people may not feel the same freedom to try to advocate for change. I need to create opportunities so they do have those avenues.

As such, this particular change leader's organization intentionally "met with the staff during two full days where we gave them this document [a new vision for change] and we invited everyone to give feedback on every single department and our vision for the future before change has even been implemented." She continued to talk about her organization's commitment to this kind of operational structure. She said: "We've always been an organization that takes the time to slow down, to reflect on, and figure out what went wrong, and how do we need to course correct. Actually, after every quarterly retreat, we have a whole reflection day where nobody goes into the office and you reflect." Stressing the importance of building relationships, another change leader said her organization includes the development of relationships in the job descriptions of her employees. She shared: "We could never ever spend enough time with people. So, there is an actual requirement that each staff member visit every single child's home four times a year. We're realistic and we set aside days and times that they are able to do that, but it's a requirement and we track it and measure it and report on it. We make it part of the job description and it's an expectation."

Several change leaders emphasized the creation of systems and structures as the primary work they do before a change is introduced. Reflecting on the start-up phase of his Christian organization that sought to change the way churches in the United States operate, this change leader said: "We said we're going to have three design constraints in our model—no paid pastors, no buildings, and 100 percent of the tithes and offerings that come in will go out to global and local missions." Also stressing a similar design focus, another change leader stated: "I think the first way is setting up the organization to be able to change and so that means being really cognizant about structural elements and ensuring that your organization is established in a way that you can have the flexibility and agility. And for us that means primarily making sure that the organization is in a posture of continuing to learn and to be willing to take bold steps when needed." Relatedly, another change leader shared her story about when she first started her organization. She reflected:

> The opportunity to start something new for me meant that we didn't have to subscribe to any of the social assumptions or historical structures of a non-profit. I don't want to create something new that is just the way things have been done and so that's how we do them. There is opportunity to structure things in a different way and to start with a clean slate and approach. So, we have not received any federal or state funding for our programs and that was intentional so that we could really think about what are the needs that we're seeing on the ground and then how do we build up programming to meet those needs based on the day-to-day data that we're collecting. That also allows us to be able to control the way we approach anything that we do to really create a culture in which everyone's input is valued from staff, leadership, and our clients. And to be agile enough to be able to create that change as we receive feedback. We need to be in a position of actually integrating feedback. Not just taking feedback, but actually having that be a part of then what we turn around and do.

In summary, catalyzing a sense of urgency for a desired change had four themes: discern the change landscape, develop relationships of trust, disrupt the current narrative, and design the organization for change. The first theme was discussed in Chapter 3 and the remaining three themes were presented throughout this chapter. Specifically, developing trust with others was an important factor in catalyzing the urgency for change. Three ways change leaders built trust were first, with a genuine curiosity about others; second, with a relentless commitment to people, place, and change itself; and third, with a proven track record of successes. Change leaders echoed these three ways of trust-building as necessary to the work of change itself, but also to the work that takes place before change is introduced. Further, disrupting the current narrative of a personal or collective story, or a particular issue or context, was necessary to fulfill change leaders' desire to facilitate relationships of deeper understanding and empathy. They believed this kind of disruption helped catalyze an urgency for change and willingly embraced discomfort for the sake of working toward a changed narrative that more accurately and broadly included the voices of those they seek to serve. Last, designing the organization for change by creating systems and structures that facilitated change, as well as continually seeking to align with a North Star, mission, guiding values, and principles served change leaders in their change endeavors.

Chapter 5

A People-Centric Approach to Connecting Others to Change

In all my years of leading change, one valuable lesson (of many!) I've learned is people are more likely to own the future they co-create with you. Working toward social change requires a social process. However, the first reality is that a competitive mindset is deeply embedded in our psyche. This mindset is counterproductive because leading change is profoundly interdependent. The second reality is that collaborating with diverse people and ways of thinking requires tremendous energy, time, and resilient commitment to the grand mission. If we're not careful, change leaders can burn out and burn bridges with others more quickly than we make progress on the change we want to see. Becoming more aware of these two realities can help change leaders approach partnership with an abundance mindset where we embrace the multiplicative power of working together with others as each person contributes their piece of genius to the change puzzle.

In response, this chapter illumines findings from change leader responses to the second research question: "In relationship with others, how do non-profit change agents connect people toward a desired change?" Change leaders were asked questions about their experiences regarding how they bring people together to join their cause, how they figure out what is most important to the people they seek to serve, and how they ensure that different groups of people feel included and valued throughout the change process. Findings are organized under four themes: (1) cultivate multivocality; (2) co-construct relational bridges; (3) center community-driven dreams; (4) create avenues for inspiration.

Theme 1: Cultivate Multivocality

All change leaders underscored the significance of including and listening to a diverse array of voices in their efforts to connect people toward a desired change. It should be noted that underlying change leaders' desire to include people throughout a change process was their deep respect for human beings, value for human dignity, and sincere desire to center

DOI: 10.4324/9781003272243-6

voices that are typically overlooked. Also, change leaders' stories continue to reflect their humility and genuine learning posture as they interact and engage with people across differences. One change leader illustrated these points well when she shared about a time when her organization intentionally made a shift to center different voices:

> Our organization used a framework of interacting that was created for a certain kind of person and for a certain kind of voice to be elevated over another's, which has continued to marginalize our margined-identity people. So, one of the shifts in helping us all move towards change in a way that is more protected, is shifting who gets centered in those conversations. So, if a particular change is going to hurt us all because it does, what we're not going to do is hurt people who are systematically already being hurt. This way of thinking moves some of the conversation to a place of considering privilege—who gets to have these conversations without impact on their bodies and who are the people having these conversations and leaving them with their bodies impacted mentally or physically in the way we carry trauma. How are we going to work to shift that so we're not piling more hurt onto people who are already having to move through the world that's going to hurt them? So, we now talk a lot about identity and a lot about margin identity, which helps us center new voices and experiences.

In order to bring people together to join their cause, change leaders expressed that communicating the reasons behind why change needed to occur was influential. When different stakeholders began to understand why change was needed and how they could make an impact, there was a stronger personal connection to a desired change. For example, one change leader stated: "Ensuring that what we're asking people to do actually adds value, and ensuring people know why what they're doing makes a difference, or the context of how that moves the bigger whole." This same change leader continued to share that this kind of communication needs to be open, consistent, and repeated "so there's always that exposure to what's happening and what that could mean," which helps people "understand the vision when it comes to point of implementation." Similarly, another change leader said that open communication creates an attractive force toward her organization's cause. She said: "I think that attracts people—just being an organization with integrity and honesty. Kind of like, 'This is who we are and we're doing the best we can and we actually need you to come alongside of us to help make it better.'"

When asked how they ensure different groups of people feel included and valued throughout the change process, a change leader stated: "I think it comes to including them in the forefront of the process." Another change leader said: "Having them be included is to really include them. So, it's really listening to a lot of people and getting advice." This same change leader also stated: "We try to involve people. It's relational, not transactional. We're in touch with people even in a personal way. So not necessarily e-blasts and those sorts of things, but picking up the phone and calling, thanking and sharing impact, getting input and feedback."

Moreover, another change leader mentioned that hiring from the specific community is an additional way to connect people toward a desired change due to the unique insight that only the community can provide: "It's prioritizing based on what we hear from the community and then what the staff thinks is best and that's why it's really imperative for me to have predominantly staff who are survivors of trauma so that they can also help to inform what is best." Similarly, yet another change leader also talked about the value of hiring context experts when she said: "We hired people because we knew that we needed them to do this work. We respect them for their backgrounds and their intellect. We don't want to hire people who we have to tell what to do all the time. Tell *us* what to do. Help *us* figure this out. I think there's so much more buy-in when we're building this together."

Likewise, another change leader stated:

> I think you've got to include them from the beginning. You've got to ask for their input and again, part of the understanding is their input doesn't guarantee that that's exactly how it's going to get shaped, but they will definitely be taken into consideration, or it becomes a dialogue. I think most of us leaders can be too impatient. This collaborative process is going to take time.

As revealed, creating spaces for dialogue was important to many change leaders as a way to connect people toward a desired change. Change leaders mentioned that dialogue was important not only to talk through the complexities of change, but to also listen and learn different people's perspectives throughout the change process. Change leaders genuinely believed in having a posture of openness toward diverse voices as well as the power of multivocality through dialogue. One change leader captured this concept when she said: "I think it's important to actually believe that even the most disruptive point of view is actually really, really valuable. I think leaders need to have a posture that seeks out the participation of different voices because everybody has a gem. That posture needs to be authentic when we affirm and facilitate participation." Another change leader said: "We've been creating dialogues. Last year, I think we had three or four weeks where we took half days to talk through questions such as, 'How do you feel about being here?; How do you feel about this from a race perspective?; How do you perceive this?;

How do you feel about that?'" Differentiating between dialogue among organizational leaders versus "people in the pews," one change leader shared:

> When it comes to working with organizational leaders or partnerships with folks who can deliver large groups of people or who have access to leverage points, I try to facilitate environments where people with many different viewpoints gather together to cross-talk with each other because I think a great thing that happens is people leave these gatherings with really different conclusions than they came with. And what's most important is that people, in their analysis, have considered and included other perspectives before arriving at a new conclusion. So, I think analysis about a problem or a change situation done in isolation is actually really dangerous. I think it's most important or more strategic to engage people in cross-talk with you before forming an analysis about a change situation. When it comes to a strategy of engaging people in the pews, part of what I try to identify is in that particular audience, what's the thing that's already a passion for them?; something that they're already motivated to do?; something that really fuels them? And then I ask myself if there's a dot, dot, dot connection to the change I'm proposing.

Dialogue spaces where change leaders both listened to and received feedback were critical to connecting people toward change. For example, a change leader stated: "I think number one is making sure that everyone understands this is an open concept. Just because we're making a change doesn't mean we still don't value you or don't value your opinion or your feedback." Another change leader also stressed the importance of receiving feedback from the people her organization serves as a way to include and connect them to change. She said: "We get feedback from those that live there to say, this is what we are, this is what we do. It's kind of an interview process both from our end and from their end, making sure that we're invited into a neighborhood and making sure that we have full participation in the neighborhoods we want to work in."

Many change leaders noted that including people along the way created a sense of ownership over the change process that helped move change forward. For example, a change leader shared a story about a time when she included different stakeholders in a fundraising gala: "In everything we do, like hosting a gala, we make sure everyone's involved because if you have a role, you own it. Ownership provides value." Likewise, another change leader reflected on the changes that were coming up in the next year and her organization's process of inclusion: "We have a lot of change coming up next year so we had workshops to empower those who are in middle management. We've given a lot of the planning to them and, as a result, there's been excitement from the employees feeling like they have more ownership of what's going to happen next year and what the goals are going to be."

In sum, cultivating multivocality was important to change leaders who desired to center marginalized voices. According to change leaders, they sought to create avenues for dialogue to ensure people felt valued and included throughout the change process. In addition, change leaders felt that multivocality added value to the organization's operational processes. Subsequently, this created a sense of ownership and empowerment for those involved.

Theme 2: Co-Construct Relational Bridges

The second theme that emerged under research question two was the importance of co-constructing relational bridges. All change leaders accentuated that relationships were the foundation for any work related to change. In fact, building relationships with others often took precedence over the work of change itself, and the timing for change initiatives depended on the rate of building relationships. Not only did change leaders authentically convey their love for people, but they were also intentional to mention that relationships were a co-constructed, reciprocally transformational phenomenon. Change leaders made relationships a priority in their work and sought to facilitate the building of relational bridges among others whenever possible. For example, a change leader said: "It's all about relationship. We're the facilitators of relationship building." Another change leader also stated: "We prioritize relationships. We have to in order to be doing this work." Similarly, one change leader declared: "So much of it has to be built on relationships and that's always a slower haul, but it's always the long-term picture." Yet another change leader expressed: "It all starts with just being in relationship with people. You need to be in relationship to people as opposed to having transactions with them."

One change leader depicted the essence of relationships when he shared a story in the context of the work he does around crisis pregnancy: "I think the most important thing in anything that's going to try to serve and change the world is that people need relationship. I think people need to be listened to and they need to be loved." This same change leader also continued to share another story of when his son asked him about a homeless man they often see: "If I'm going to help the guy, I need to get out of my car, plan to set aside a couple of hours, go sit down with him, start to build a real relationship, and see if I can use my network to help him." Interestingly, another change leader mentioned the term "god conscience" as a way to describe the opposite of a co-constructed relational bridge. He said:

Have you ever heard of the term "god conscience?" It's interesting because when we give wrong and when we do ministry wrong, we obviously harm others, but what's not so obvious is that we also actually harm ourselves. I have an aunt who likes to give stuff to people who live at a particular Indian reservation. What she's actually doing is she's creating what's called a god conscience where she believes that, without her, these people wouldn't be able to survive. That mindset just perpetuates poverty is what it does. In a lot of ways, you can become like a god to others by just providing material resources at a distance. Rather, almost all change has to deal with some type of poverty of relationship. People need relationship.

Similarly, another change leader talked about the shift her organization has made to prioritize the co-construction of relational bridges and human connections. She said: "I think we're trying to do things differently too where we're choosing to rely on that personal relationship rather than what we have to do. I have to do a lot of redefining what success is. It's highly relational and we work really hard to establish those very human connections."

The co-construction of relational bridges required a lot of listening. Also mentioned under research question one, the act of listening was mentioned here by all change leaders as one of the most important acts that takes place in the work they do to connect people to change. Listening helped change leaders figure out what was most important to the people they serve. For example, a change leader said: "You listen. You listen to their stories and you share your own." Also, another change leader mentioned: "I think a lot of times it's just listening and forming those relationships." Moreover, yet another change leader stated: "But the way that I make sure our programming is meeting a need is that I go and I listen to them and I talk to them. I hear what they do and know their lives." One change leader shared a story about how he spends time in brothels in order to understand the needs of the people he serves. He said: "We've spent a lot of time trying to figure out what their greatest needs are. We have done different things like just simply being in the brothels on a daily basis and trying to understand what their most significant needs are from the outside looking in." Another change leader also shared that learning about needs of people "just happens" when you're in genuine relationship with them. She said: "It's through observing, it's through listening, it's through being in relationships. Through relationships, we feel needs, we listen to needs, we see needs." And another change leader also underscored the act of listening during a time when his organization was developing a partnership bridge with multiple other stakeholders across the Chicagoland area. He said:

We had to do a massive amount of mutual education and listening and sharing, for them to teach us: Who are you? Where did you live? What is life? And for us to teach them: Who are we? Where do we live? And what is life? We take what we've learned through listening, and use it to develop an initiative, or a concept, which is eventually presented back to different stakeholders for more feedback. We listen some more by asking: Do you think this initiative or concept would work and how would it not work? Based on their feedback, we refine and change the concept until we end up with the successful change initiatives we have today.

Change leaders also communicated that relational bridge-building was critical to generating greater impact and ripples of change beyond the communities on which they focused. In fact, developing partnership bridges was mentioned by most change leaders as critical to the work of connecting people toward a desired change. Noteworthy is change leaders' emphasis on having a learning posture when developing partnerships as well as their recognition that the work of change cannot be done solo. One change leader said: "Learning from our local partners again, that's probably the most important piece. Just recognizing that you need people in order to do this work." Another change leader stated: "We partner with other existing organizations that are here long term that have specific initiatives." Moreover, yet another change leader mentioned: "We work in partnership. We don't do our work alone. A lot of it is done in coalition so it's not like our organization's cause alone. It's so much bigger cause than that." One change leader's reflection illustrated the learning posture of her organization when she shared: "I would say that we're a continuous learning organization. It's working *with* the people, not doing something *for* them or doing something *to* them but kind of working through it with them, which is really time intensive, but it's the only way to do it." Another change leader referenced the reciprocity of partnership bridges when she stated: "I think the gift of the partnership is that it's reciprocal and it's mutual. We want to be people who aren't just taking and aren't just giving. There needs to be some back and forth." One change leader talked about how her organization calls partnership building "bridging the gap." She shared:

We call that "bridging the gap" and it's very much a strategy and something that we're really intentional about. First of all, communicating to the staff that we want to be bridge builders. That may mean we're being a bridge builder across culture, language, and socioeconomic status, but that we all need to develop those relationships for everyone to work together for the cause.

As bridge builders, change leaders thought collective impact was increasingly possible. One change leader captured this thought when she shared about her organization's "collective impact strategy." She said that she brings "a lot of different players to the table. A lot of known and unknown partners and really thinks about that collective impact. We want to make sure that we're constantly and very intentionally working with our partners for this kind of collective impact." Another change leader beautifully illustrated the dignity of partnership bridges when she said: "In the communities where we work we're partnering with the people who are most respected in the community and are really those ambassadors or those beacons of change. These are the people all others in the community respect."

Some change leaders specifically mentioned that partnership bridges were necessary in the work toward systemic change. One change leader conveyed: "I think finding the partners within, that's a long-term process for systems change, but when you do have the partners willing to put the effort in, then the results are really good." Another change leader also talked about systemic change and said: "You can't just make systemic change as an individual and you can't just make systemic change as an organization. It has to be a very collaborative thing. We've partnered up with not just local organizations but also national organizations that are addressing systemic issues."

In sum, change leaders insisted that building relational bridges needed to be co-constructed and not only unidirectional. This way, relationship building honored and respected the dignity of each party's agency to go deeper at one's own pace. Partnership bridges were important to change leaders because of the increased potential for collective impact that could influence ripples of change through systemic layers.

Theme 3: Center Community-Driven Dreams

The third theme that emerged was centering community-driven dreams. Most change leaders communicated great desire to see the expression and flourishing of the hopes and dreams of those they serve. Beneath this desire was a humble awareness of every human's power and ability, especially when given equitable opportunities. As such, change leaders articulated that they viewed the people they served as the "heroes" and themselves more as "guides." One change leader specifically used this language when he said: "We're not trying to put ourselves in place of hero, but, we're just saying God has called us to be with our neighbors and walk with them. So, our job is the guide." Another change leader also used similar language when she reflected on our human instincts to be a hero: "When helping becomes insistent then I'm tapping into my need to be the hero." This same change leader continued to talk about how being more of a guide in the change process was birthed from a deep respect for human dignity:

> And this goes back to beyond trust. It's about respecting the autonomy and dignity of the other person. It's so easy when we're genuinely excited about something that's helped us and sometimes in our enthusiasm to share that with other people, it comes across as, "Well, you have to do this, or this is the only way forward."

As change leaders took this posture of guide, several change leaders mentioned that they operated under the radar so that the spotlight shone on those they served. For example, one change leader said: "A lot of what we do, nobody knows that we do it. We do it very subtly, behind the scenes, which is what I like—under the radar." Also, another change leader stated:

> I often tell people that I think in order to have real change you have to be willing to take the backseat. People may never even realize I exist or that I was a part of the conversation and I have to be okay with that. I might play into all of the work but somebody else might take all of the credit.

While working under the radar, change leaders shared that supporting the dreams of others was their priority because of their genuine belief that leaders within the communities in which they served were better equipped as change experts for their specific contexts. They believed that local change agents made great impact. For example, one change leader stated: "I did see how the local solutions really made a difference." Another change leader clearly explained this point when she said:

> The experts on their situation, are people in that situation. You don't learn about it from textbooks. You don't learn about it from some professor somewhere. You sit with people over and over again and you listen to their stories. They're the experts on their own lives. They're the experts on what change they want to see in their lives. They're the experts on what it will take for that change to happen. Then we determine what we're going to do because the community knows what change they want to see.

As change leaders worked alongside the context experts in the communities, one change leader passionately declared the paradigm shift that's necessary for change agents to do that well: "What if we changed the paradigm to—we're not just pursuing whatever we dream because we could fund it, but that we actually support the dreams of the leaders who are already here. They could do it better." In addition, another change leader mentioned that goals and dreams should be client- or community-driven. She said: "We're community driven. Our solutions are fully inspired, implemented, managed by our community partners. So, they're going to feel valued because they're the ones doing it and they own it completely and they're actually even paying for it." Another change leader also talked about client-led work when she shared: "Our belief is in client-led work. We're not an organization that feels it's appropriate for us to dictate to the client what they should want. Once you're our client, our job is to serve you." This same change leader continued to express: "I think we're definitely talking to people on the ground, and understanding how it's playing out. And then working with them in partnership to figure out, well what's the solution that would actually help you."

In sum, change leaders declared that centering community-driven dreams was their goal. In order to accomplish that, change leaders embraced their role as guides and sought the expertise of the community members to work toward the change they desired for themselves and their respective contexts.

Theme 4: Create Avenues for Inspiration

The final theme under the second research question that emerged from interviews was the value of creating avenues for inspiration that motivated others to connect to a desired change. Most change leaders repeatedly said they inspired people toward change by communicating their organization's vision and mission. Communication was based on motivational needs of different stakeholders, as one change leader expressed about her volunteers: "We use a model to understand how our volunteers are motivated. Some are motivated by relationship, some are motivated by power and data. We communicate with them differently based on what we think will hook them." Change leaders did not hesitate to convey that people connect to change as leaders "gravitate people toward a mission." Another change leader mentioned: "It is making sure that everybody who is a part of your organization, whether that person is a volunteer or a board member or staff member, understands what your mission is and where you're going and why it's important—why their piece of the pie is important." Gravitating people toward a vision and mission was also important to this change leader as she shared:

> I think it begins with vision. Sometimes people rally behind a person, but that's not really good. You don't want them rallying behind a person. What you really want is people to rally behind a vision because that's what brings long-term commitment. People will let you down. Even great leaders will let you down. Leaders are going to

come and go over time. But what you really want is people to rally behind a mission, a cause.

Another change leader shared a similar insight, stressing that a "good" and clear vision or mission helps diffuse the communication of that vision or mission so that more people are drawn in: "I think our vision, our mission drive bringing people together, especially if you have a good vision and a good mission that really clearly articulate what you're doing and how you're doing it." Another change leader also declared that clarity was critical when he said: "I think you have to have a clear mission. I think it needs to be easily understood. I think the important thing to do is to tell people what you're changing and why." Yet another change leader similarly articulated the significance of communicating "why" when she stated:

> I believe you can plan for change in a way that makes sense to people and gets people on board by making it easier for people to understand the why. If people understand why you are changing or why you're shifting directions, then (a) it makes them feel less anxious about the change, and (b) it can reinvigorate them and make them strong proponents of the change, or (c) it'll just make them understand that they don't want to be a part of this change and then they'll get off the bus, out of the way.

Similarly, another change leader focused his reflection on his client stakeholder base when he said: "For our clients who come in, same thing. We've got client orientation and we just talk about why we exist."

Many change leaders talked about the motivation and inspiration that comes from being a part of something significant *with* and *for* a collective of other people. However, one change leader said that believing in significance rather than success takes a paradigm shift. He said:

> Some of it's around what we talked about a little earlier about getting people to think more about being significant than being successful. Success is about your own accomplishments; significance is about the accomplishments of other people. Not all successful people are significant. And if you get people to start to think about that and what it means to leverage their success, the world changes tomorrow.

Another change leader gave a beautiful illustration of how collective work inspires, motivates, and connects people toward change, also noting that leaders often create avenues of inspiration: "I pictured myself getting out of the car, trying to push it, and then immediately being

surrounded by people who want to join in that cause of moving it together. There's something compelling about knowing that together we
can effect change. So as leaders, we hold up our flag to say, 'Let's go! We
can do this.'" Moreover, another change leader shared that there is a
need to reimagine a movement of change that inspires people: "I think a
lot of what I'm trying to do is to architect a way to nudge a movement
that's already in motion and to figure out how to inspire others."

As both change leaders referenced above, other change leaders were
quick to note that people are inspired by movements of change that are
working and visibly making a difference. Another example of this includes one change leader's testimony when he shared about the time
when his organization first began to reach out to serve the homeless
population: "The other thing that had happened was when the surrounding areas saw what we were doing, they said, 'Hey, we could do
that too.' The movement had really taken hold." Other change leaders
shared that communicating stories of impact was critical to inspiring and
connecting people toward change by tapping common human emotions.
For example, one change leader shared: "I think I've learned that in the
power of story, it's not necessarily the issue that you can connect with,
but it's the common feelings of humanity that we've all dealt with,
whether it be shame or rejection or violence in different forms."
Moreover, another change leader talked about how she constantly
communicates stories and images of impact to audiences across the
world, but how it's just as crucial to share those same stories with her
staff and others who may not be the mouthpiece for storytelling. She
said: "So just constantly trying to remember to share those stories with
our team. We capture those stories of impact so that I constantly inspire
people and build trust and solidarity and have people feel like they are a
part of a family when they're with our organization."

Further, change leaders revealed that the hope derived from celebra-
tions, affirmations, or other positive language used intentionally to encourage and inspire others helped connect people toward a desired change.
For change leaders, these acts of hope were simple yet powerful ways to
connect people to change. It should be noted that change leaders were very
much aware of the power of positive language and were intentional with
its use, which included awareness of the timing, audience, and mode of
communication. For instance, one change leader stated: "Critiquing
people is not the way to get them to change. It's actually applauding them
when they do even a small thing that's in the right direction. Definitely
thanking people and thanking them publicly." Another change leader also
shared about how she celebrates the leaders with whom she works:

> I would say celebrating along the way. Reaching out personally and
> thanking them. Being a cheerleader. So much of what happens in

leadership goes unnoticed and that's fine to a degree, but it's also great to notice people and say, "I can't believe you guys pulled that off," and "It's made such a difference in your city and your people."

Yet another change leader who works in historically violent neighborhoods, specifically focused her inspiration story on how she intentionally communicates hopeful responses to the reality that's before them in order to motivate others and connect them to change. She shared: "I think also just this sense of being hopeful. I think really having a hopeful response of, 'Hey, we can do this,' is what gets people excited. A clear vision is important and then that hopeful response that we can do this." Similarly, another change leader who also works with people who have experienced violence, stated that affirming language connects people toward change, but sometimes that language has to be modeled to those whose reality might be the opposite: "It's important to practice affirmation, which is not normal in our communities. I'd say they're not used to that, so it's teaching them how to affirm. Modeling affirmation first. That's how they learn to affirm others."

In summary, connecting people toward a desired change had four themes: cultivate multivocality, co-construct relational bridges, center community-driven dreams, and create avenues for inspiration. Undergirding much of these themes were change leaders' values for human dignity and agency as well as an awareness of their personal potential contributions amidst the context expertise of local change agents who were already doing social change work in their communities. Change leaders communicated the need to include a diverse spectrum of voices all throughout a change process; not only listening to what people had to say, but also integrating and acting on feedback received. In addition, change leaders intentionally used language and partnerships to co-construct relational bridges that were reciprocally transformative. They continued to express a desire to be inclusive as well as to have a learning posture in relationship with others. Moreover, change leaders invested significant time and energy toward centering the dreams of others by listening to the hopes and desires of the people they serve and guiding them toward a new reality. Change leaders also mentioned that centering the dreams of others involved taking the lead from others rather than prescribing a formula for action. Finally, change leaders created ways for others to be inspired through not only communicating a clear and meaningful vision and mission, but also rallying others toward collective action and sharing hopeful impact stories along the way.

Chapter 6

A People-Centric Approach to Continuing Momentum for Change

Ever since I was a middle schooler, I wanted to change the world. In fact, my grandfather who helped raise me for the first several years of my life was an entrepreneur. He introduced the Singer sewing machine into South Korea and changed the way women worked and contributed to the South Korean economy. In a patriarchal culture, that was a big deal. Even as a young girl, my grandfather intentionally took me on work trips and shared stories about his change leadership strategies. In his own way, and as an expression of his love for me, he equipped me and left a change leadership legacy. He's definitely my inspiration in my change leadership endeavors today. Just like my grandfather, people-centric change leaders are very aware that continuing momentum for change involves thinking about *who* will carry that momentum forward. Leading change is a privilege that extends beyond ourselves. Sure, each one of us can make a powerful impact through our change leadership. However, we get to multiply that impact exponentially by intentionally leading change with others and sustaining change for generations to come.

Providing a unique view on sustainability, this section illumines findings from change leader responses to the third research question: "In relationship with others, how do non-profit change agents continue momentum for a desired change?" Change leaders were asked questions about their experiences regarding how they helped people learn to change, and the work that needs to take place when they implement change so that it lasts over time. Finally, change leaders were asked to imagine that they have been leading a movement of change for 10 to 30 years and what they did to sustain the movement for so long. Findings are organized under four themes: (1) seek teamwork; (2) surrender control; (3) shape cultural practices within organization; (4) steward care and development of others.

Theme 1: Seek Teamwork

All change leaders thought that the key to continuing momentum for a desired change was assembling the right team of people around them. In

DOI: 10.4324/9781003272243-7

fact, one change leader stated: "It's surrounding yourself with the right people." They sought to build teams for their respective movements through the right hires, board members, and friends, as well as the next generation of leaders. For example, a change leader shared: "Number one is build a team. I have a wonderful team of leaders who have been here for more than ten years. So, we're in this together. We're pulling together. When one person gets tired or wants to quit, the others pull us along." Change leaders continued to repeat a keen awareness that they could not do the work they do alone, and relationships remained to be an important piece to continuing momentum for a desired change.

There was an overwhelming response from change leaders regarding the necessity to hire the right people. First, change leaders expressed that hiring the right people meant hiring for complementary skill as well as for character. One change leader summed it up well when she said: "I have an awesome team, they're the best. They are all A players, super compassionate, they work really, really hard and I have 100 percent confidence in all of them." Another change leader also stated: "I think it's important to have smart people on staff. I have been blessed with attracting smart and creative talent. An organization is about the people and if you don't have good people with strong skill sets, you don't succeed." Like most other change leaders, one particular change leader underscored the importance of having a learning posture: "We have been committed to learn what we need to learn and have been willing to be the novice in the room, to ask all the silly questions and be willing to be wrong in many ways. But then we also make sure we're getting people around us, on our team who are experts in their area." Another change leader said that she constantly asks questions about building out her team: "And then of course just the practical things like who's going to be on our board? Who's going to be the next executive director? Who can we hire? Those are just the regular organizational things you have to think about." Yet another change leader stated:

> You have to surround yourself with people who complement you, and with team members who complement each other. Your capacity can only be so big, right? But if you surround yourself with people who have different and complementary expertise, then what happens is you get the magical mix of all their brain power, all your brain power, all our heart power into the process, which results in outcomes that are better than what one person or a group of really similar people could come up with.

Similarly, another change leader shared that the team he surrounds himself with will determine both the present and the future impact of his organization. He said: "We're only as good as our team. So, we've been very specific in trying to get people who are very good at what they do in their particular area."

Change leaders also said that hiring the right people involved looking for hires who fit their organization's culture. One change leader said: "I think we've done a really good job hiring the right people and weeding out those that don't fit our culture and climate." Likewise, another change leader used DNA to talk about his organization's culture, stating:

> I think that over time as an organization, you should start to better understand what the DNA of a team member of yours should be. We have five team pillars: relationships, energy, edge, limitless, and simplicity. An interesting exercise is when I'm interviewing somebody, I'll simply communicate those five words to a candidate and ask them to start talking about each one. This way, I learn very quickly whether a candidate can talk about those words and what they mean to them. I can gain more clarity around this candidate's potential to meet our organizational needs. Regardless of who I end up hiring, I will also develop the person into our culture and help them navigate our culture so they can eventually manage themselves.

One change leader noted that when he hired for cultural fit, his employees stayed longer in the organization, which helped continue momentum for change. He said: "We have the best staff in this county. But I love that we have developed a corporate culture around here. That in the thirty years we've done business, we have had one person who left to take another job."

In addition, many change leaders considered their community partners as well as the people they serve as essential parts of their team. Change leaders strategically hired from the communities in which they served as a way to continue momentum for change long-term. In fact, one change leader said: "We need to have people who are on our staff and board who represent the community—that is so vital." More often than not, change leaders interchanged stories of community hires with their hopes to raise up the next generation of leaders for their respective movements. For example, one change leader shared: "The final thing is that we've hired from the community. Part of our model is developing the next generation of leaders and I see my organization as a platform for those young people to come back and change their community." This change leader continued to state: "We really do see our work as a platform for young people to change their communities and that has always been our model. I think that's why our work's been sustainable this long and it's something I'm not willing to give up." Hiring from the community was reflected in many change leader stories. For example, another change leader stated: "We hired from the community. They're really core to who we are. We have board members from the neighborhood and most of our staff live in the community or are from this community or one similar to it. It matters who you place around you—your board and staff leadership." Also, another change leader reflected on the concept of sustainability as the need to engage her community when she said: "I think the biggest thing has been constantly recruiting advocates and supporters and making sure that the pipeline is never dry. I think that's honestly the biggest thing." Another change leader summed up teamwork well when she shared:

> I think you need three things. First, you need an engaged community; second, you need strong institutions; and third, you need individual leaders and actors. The reason you need all three is (I've seen this across movements) that individual folks can be amazingly powerful. Their individual story is powerful, but unless they're a very unique leader, they tend to burn out. They alone cannot be responsible for a movement. Then you need engaged communities because it's not a movement if it's just a couple of people doing all the work. We have to capture the imagination and be aligned values-wise with other people for that piece. And then the third piece is institutions, because we are here hopefully for a long time. Ideally, we are working to put ourselves out of business. In an ideal world, no one would need our services, right? Social change takes a long time.

Other change leaders had a more general focus on developing leaders as a way to continue momentum for change. One change leader said: "Recognizing you can't do it alone, and making sure that other people are as vested as you or close enough, and constantly looking for those next generation of people, whoever they may be in whatever capacity." Another change leader reflected:

> I have to create an organization of leaders. The more they can become owners of the organization as a movement and the more I can lead them to become decision makers, I think that's going to be required for long-term sustainability. We are creating the kind of leaders that can think and develop and lead and build their own organizations.

Another change leader expressed that she develops leaders not by training them to know certain things, but, rather, by "passing on a pedagogy" that helps others know how to be change agents who can wisely move change forward. Similarly, another change leader also talked about how she was influenced by a model she saw on a service trip to Honduras that she has adopted to train and develop leaders in the work she does with her clients who live in poverty:

Rather than training people today to do ABC specific jobs, we're training them to have skills of creativity, problem-solving, and building interpersonal relationships. These skills are going to transfer to every industry, and as industries automate, those people skills become more important because that's how you differentiate yourself from an automated worker. And so, I think a lot about how we don't fall into the trap of what's attractive today, but really think about long term value. How are we best serving our community and our constituents to prepare them for what is going to be effective in ten years so that the time they invest today isn't just for the next three years but they've been equipped with the tools and the learning to propel themselves beyond that point?

Last, many change leaders mentioned that accountability to and for a team of people was critical to continuing momentum for change because change requires so much learning.

Change leaders shared that not only did they need to keep different groups of people accountable in the change implementation process, but they also needed others to keep them accountable. In fact, one change leader stated: "I think the biggest thing to stay in a change is accountability." Again, change leaders' stories about accountability reflected their commitment to both consistent communication and relationships. One change leader enthusiastically proclaimed that accountability was the key to sustainability. She expressed: "Accountability. So that's what's coming to my mind of things that we've changed and we've kept them going and its accountability. It's just holding people accountable to what the change is." This change leader continued her story to include more insight into change and her commitment to see change through. Her story also reflects an awareness that many change leaders shared, which was the awareness of time and the amount of patience it takes for the change agent to do the work necessary for change to last over time. She said:

> I know that when we're changing something, I have to set aside time to make sure that it's changing and it's operating how it's supposed to be. And it takes a while to work out. Change is hard. Some people do well, some people don't, and some people just keep going back to the old ways. Again, accountability is critical and also understanding that change takes time and that you're going to have to continue to pour into that change until it's running like clockwork, until it's where you want it to be and that depends on the change sometimes. It takes a while to do that.

Another change leader who works with victims of sexual or domestic abuse reflected more on keeping the community accountable to change when she shared:

> We think about how to hold communities and people accountable. We're engaging and talking about the issue and we're helping those community members that want to be helpful figure out how they could be helpful, and we push them to take stock of what's happening around them and to be accountable and make those changes.

As previously mentioned, relationships continued to have a big emphasis in the conversations around accountability. Change leaders repeatedly said that accountability to and with a team of people was housed in deep relationships with others. In fact, in her reflection on how change lasts over time, one change leader said: "I would say relational support, solid relational support and mentorship because that creates accountability. So, I think that's it—the accountability." Also thinking about accountability, another change leader said: "I'm gonna say it again—I think it's a people approach. I think I've talked to people, I've made sure that I'm in spaces and made sure that I've built relationships—like equal relationships, not just like I-need-something-from-you relationships, but like true relationships." Continuing her story, this change leader connected her thoughts to sustainability. She said: "And so I think if I see myself in the next ten years really sustaining a movement, it's because I've built relationships. It's because I've advocated for a movement. It's because of the people, because I've been around people and really engaged people." Likewise, when asked what she did to sustain a movement of change over time, another change leader said: "I committed to relationship with my coworkers in a really deep, intentional way. I committed to prioritizing that above the work. A continual commitment to our partners and relationship."

In essence, change leaders said they needed a team to keep them accountable to learning, growing, and even resting—again revealing their humility and their awareness of self-care as one way to sustain change. First, this required change leaders to admit and accept that personal change was necessary. For example, one change leader stated: "I think the first thing you have to identify is that there's a lot of room for transformation. You have to admit it first. Then you have to say it out loud so that people hear you, will want to help you, and want to hold you accountable." Including friends as part of her team, another change leader said: "Sometimes it's just having really good friends that you could call and say, 'Hey, I'm going to be doing this or that for work.' And you've got good friends that can say, 'No, tonight you're going to go to the movies with us.' That can help you." Similar to other responses, another change leader shared her need for "accountability to recognize pride and ego" so that she could keep her focus on the purpose of her mission. Likewise, yet another change leader talked about how his team keeps him accountable to his mission by sustaining him in his work:

> Collaboration and doing this journey with people is critical. If this is an individual journey where I'm just this isolated person leading the masses, it's easy to get cynical when you're by yourself. It's easy to get burned out when you're isolated. When you're in community, other people lift you up when you're down and vice versa. Even the defeats are better in community because you're there together and you're in it together and you're going to be there fighting together the next day.

Further, another change leader mentioned that friends and family keep her accountable to her mission by providing a means for self-sustaining renewal. She shared: "A couple of years ago I started surfing with my husband and I've never loved anything so much that I'm so bad at. But I just really do lose track of time with that. I also think deep conversations with good friends renew me for the work ahead."

In sum, this theme of seeking teamwork was important to sustaining the momentum for change over time. Change leaders had long-term perspectives when creating teams and were thoughtful in ensuring that future leaders were developed to carry the torch. Change leaders sought to surround themselves with diverse teams who kept them accountable as well as provided means for self-care.

Theme 2: Surrender Control

The second theme under continuing momentum for change was the insight that change leaders could not possibly control change nor the momentum for it. It is worthwhile to note that although their work was weighty, change leaders, in their wisdom, did not carry the burden of changing the world on their shoulders. This recognition came from a discerned awareness of their own capacities as well as a long-term perspective of change itself. Change leaders also learned along the way that change cannot and should not be controlled, or it might become harmful and damaging to the very people they want to serve. Finally, this recognition and awareness did not distract or subtract from the hard, sacrificial, joyful, and committed work that change agents willingly and humbly engaged in every day.

First, many change leaders shared how they were intentional to not create a movement or an organization that was dependent on them through continued partnership with others "on the ground" who were viewed as collaborators for change rather than competitors. Change leaders continued to express that the release of control over a movement into the hands of as many people as possible would be the best way to sustain change over time. Also, one change leader said: "The mission will not suffer because I walk away." Another change leader said: "I never want it to be dependent on me." Yet another change leader shared: "We very much are trying to ensure that this is not tied to any particular personality of my wife or I—making sure that it's not dependent upon us so that someone else can step in and continue to lead and run. So, if this continues on for generations beyond us we consider that a huge win to have that continued impact." Another change leader voiced a similar story when he shared about a time when his current organization gave birth to another one. He considered leading the new organization but decided it would be better on its own: "It's not about us holding on to everything, it's about us releasing and letting go."

All change leaders who identified as Christian in their beliefs expressed their desire to surrender control because God was the ultimate initiator and sustainer of change. One change leader stated: "God can change the city, but we're gonna need to shine our light. I always know that this is God's thing and God will sustain it." Another change leader said: "If God wants this, He'll have it until He doesn't want it anymore." As such, Christian change leaders shared that they partner with God in God's movement of change in the world, and as they do so, they prioritize their commitment to God because they derive their strength and wisdom from Him. One change leader described a time when she surrendered control after a really long and difficult day of change-making:

> There are a lot of things that are super strategic, super important. A lot of things that are really urgent, but I think there's important work, especially of a leader, of discerning if this is the particular thing that God is inviting me to pick up now for this time? I felt tremendously released to surrender my work to God. It was such a heavy emotional thing that I was carrying for several weeks and I felt like we did what we were supposed to do. And after you do what you're supposed to do, then you release it to God because He's got the bigger story that He's knitting together.

Also, change leaders talked a lot about releasing control through prayer as their primary way of sustaining change within themselves as well as in the world. One change leader said she learned to think this way from a conversation she had with the theologian Desmond Tutu when she asked him how he was able to remain joyful in his old age despite the violence he witnessed as an anti-apartheid and human rights activist in his native country of South Africa. His response to her question was prayer. She shared: "If I do anything right for the next thirty years, of course there's multiple things with strategy and structure, the right people, the right board, funding strategies and the right processes. But I think what all of that is still derived from would be prayer." Another change leader also talked about the important role prayer has in his work. He shared an example of a conversation he has with God every morning:

> I have a very high sense of responsibility and if I'm not careful, I can try and take responsibility for what is not mine to be responsible for. And so, I have to continually pray, "Okay, God I need to put this back into Your hands because You have not created me to be responsible for this. You're responsible for this." And I don't say that as if I'm pointing my finger at God, like "You're responsible!" but in a genuine posture of release from my hands so that I'm surrendering an unhealthy control.

Another change leader talked more about how her organization has a culture of prayer so they can grow in their ability to release control and redirect when necessary: "We have a culture of prayer. We also have a ten-year plan. I'm holding it very loosely to know that none of it may happen because all of a sudden something completely different can happen. And we'll have to learn to adjust to that and redirect."

Christian change leaders also confidently expressed they could release control because they knew God would provide for their needs. For example, one change leader stated: "I stay true to what I'm committed to do and I'm gonna trust that every day, God's gonna provide. I'm going to do my best. And to be a voice. As I do my very best work, I trust that God will send the right people at the right time." In addition, another change leader shared about his perspective on his organization's fundraising galas:

> So at our recent gala, there was a family that gave $130,000 this year. And if that family decides that for the next three years they're not in, we don't make our goal. I can go and try to convince that family, but God's got to order and convict their hearts to give or not. I trust that God will provide the funds we need either through this family or elsewhere.

In sum, theme 2 of surrendering control centered around change leaders' reflections of not wanting the work of change to be dependent upon them. As much as possible, change leaders sought to empower others to sustain change, which stemmed from their awareness that they should not and could not bear the responsibility of change on their own. In particular, the Christian change leaders in this study stressed the significance of remembering that God is the author and sustainer of all change.

Theme 3: Shape Cultural Practices within Organization

The third theme that surfaced from change leader stories was the need to shape cultural practices within their organizations in order to continue momentum for change. Most change leaders mentioned that their organization's cultural values centered around communication or relationships, and that it was not only important to design one's organization for change as mentioned under research question one, but to also continue to shape cultural practices and rhythms in the organization so that change is anchored within the organizational culture. In fact, a change leader said: "The most important part of what we do going forward is creating a consistent culture. Like having values, building them from the ground up, and having our leaders sit with them so our values become a part of their DNA. You cultivate that." Another change leader expressed her vision of continuing momentum for change through her organization: "I think you have to build in cultural practices and rhythms that reinforce and support the new change. And you have to particularly pay attention to the cultural practices that were part of the old thing that you're trying to leave and make sure that you rightly and appropriately dismantle those." One change leader stated that when others outside of his organization can articulate his organization's values as a result of their lived experience with the organization, he feels the most hopeful that the momentum for change will continue: "How I know this is working is if I go to the person at the fringe of your neighborhood and they can articulate our values. It's okay if they don't have the right language and terminology, but they can articulate them because these values are the most essential part of their experience."

Some change leaders talked about anchoring culture change by consistently being willing to talk about and receive feedback on the expression of cultural values. For example, one change leader stated: "We always survey the staff about how we are doing in communication because communication is a high priority. We're constantly working on that to try to be better." Another change leader said that he also consistently talks about cultural values and also seeks to make every decision in alignment with them. He shared a story of how he scaled his organization by seeking to live out his cultural values:

> There are six words that really mean a lot to me—brand, culture, effective, efficient, scalable, and sustainable. We started out of my garage and with a very big goal that we were going to expand by building one site in every major city in the country. And we talk about that daily. Everything we do has to do with that. Decisions we make have to do with that.

Similarly, another change leader shared that her organization seeks to be a workplace with open communication as well as a place that lives out what they teach to their clients, who are low-income students and teachers. Here, she shared a story of how they practice what they value: "We talk a lot about mindsets with our students and with our teachers and I think that is very much aligned with what we do with our staff. Sometimes we have to change our own mindsets and call each other out when we see that we're not doing that." Shaping and anchoring cultural practices within an organization requires a lot of continued learning. One change leader gave this insight: "Two-thirds of all organizational change initiatives fail. There was a theme with the one-third where the change initiatives really took root and gained momentum. The theme was a relentless commitment to being a learning culture."

Change leaders also talked about shaping cultural practices in the context of fundraising. Several change leaders mentioned that their organization had a philosophy around fundraising that became a cultural practice as a way to accomplish their ultimate change missions. These stories also reflect their commitment to being a learning organization. For example, a change leader stated: "A part of that sustainability is making sure that we're building out financial models so that we get enough revenue coming in both through donations, but then also sales revenue of product that will allow us to continue to move forward." Likewise, another change leader had to change his funding model to continue momentum for change as well: "We have to change our funding model so that we're not dependent solely on money from places that kind of tie our hands. We started thinking about the need to have a diversity of revenue streams." Yet another change leader also shared her strategy around fundraising and what she communicates to her staff as a cultural practice:

> I think a lot of people misunderstand the relationship between a donor and an organization because you're not out there begging or pleading or asking for money. That's not it. You're actually providing a service. The donor is a person who cares about certain communities, cares about certain issues—they want to see change. You're the agent that's going to create that change. They've got a day job or maybe they're vacationing in Hawaii. And they just want to know someone's doing the job. You are an investment for them, in their own philanthropic goal, right? They're your partner. And hopefully a good partner in that they respect your expertise and they want you to do good work and they trust you. And those are the kinds of donors you ideally want.

Surprisingly, another change leader talked about how the healthy integration of work with family was important for him to stay the course over the long term. He shared this insight in the context of a bigger story of how he decided to take his donors on rock-climbing trips as a way to thank them for their generosity. He and his wife are avid rock climbers, and as a married couple, they spent a lot of time rock climbing together to nurture their marriage. As such, he has decided to integrate this life-giving activity into his organization's culture as a way to also invite and spend time with his wife. He shared:

> We get to construct the culture we want and I want to construct a culture that really provides for my family and for me in the end as well, so that it's a thriving place that is full of life. It would probably be different if it was somebody else—maybe they would do a lot of hockey games or baseball games or something. But I wanted to construct it so that it fits my heart and I'm able to integrate that. For my family.

In sum, theme 3 of shaping cultural practices within an organization in order to sustain the momentum for change took various forms. Change leaders often mentioned the importance of aligning action with organizational values by creating practices that would act as pillars of remembrance for the changes they hoped would continue over time.

Theme 4: Steward Care and Development of Others

Stewarding the care and development of others was the fourth theme under the research question of how change agents continue momentum for change. This theme transpired primarily from the interview question of how change leaders help others learn to change. Surprisingly, when asked this question, many change leaders expressed joy and awe at the opportunity to answer it. In fact, a change leader said: "That's a really cool question!" Change leaders naturally connected change to learning and learning to change, and generally had the perspective that it was a privilege to care for and develop others for future significance. As such, change leaders did not hesitate to share wisdom and ideas regarding processes they have witnessed to be life-changing for those they serve.

First, many change leaders mentioned that helping people learn to change needs to be grounded in the self-motivation and learning posture of the individual. As one change leader put it, people need to be "open to wanting to align, to wanting to grow." In terms of helping her staff learn to change, another change leader said: "We hire people who want to grow as people and as professionals." Similarly, yet another change leader said: "I think the main thing is believing that you can; that life can be different." One change leader shared that the children he serves encourage him with their desire to learn: "While I continuously see the lack of book ownership in these children's homes, the good news is they are really eager to be better readers. They want to learn, they are excited, but they just don't own any books at home." Another change leader also stated: "I think one of the things that makes the most successful client is the client who comes to us with an understanding that they need to create change in their life." Likewise, yet another change leader declared: "You gotta be woke enough to understand that you need to change. I can't do anything if people don't walk in the door and say, 'Hey, we want to change.'" In the same way, another change leader said: "I can't make somebody change. However, I can create a little bit of soil around them that would make them believe again, that change is possible." One change leader also said: "And I think in a lot of ways, it's important that no matter what age someone is, to be open to change and learn what needs to be unlearned and relearned."

In addition, many change leaders said that caring for and developing others required facilitating a lot of hard, honest, and uncomfortable conversations. One change leader shared a story about a time when she had to facilitate a misunderstanding between her employees. However, she viewed it as a necessary learning opportunity for mutual growth and learning. She said:

> We have an African American employee who's from the community my organization serves. He's been with us for a very long time. And we have a Caucasian woman we hired who's from outside of the community and has been here for only a year and a half. Recently, they had a miscommunication about race. So, how do we get them to grow? How we all grow together is we get in a room and talk about that miscommunication. That can't fester. That becomes toxic. So, we had to have a conversation. We do a lot of talking, a lot of facilitated conversations. We do a lot of apologizing. We have a lot of grace here for every single thing.

Sometimes the uncomfortable conversations involved communicating something disruptive enough to motivate someone to change. For example, a change leader stated: "How do I disrupt people enough so that they'll start doing something different and so we can see something different happen? I think somebody has got to nudge them and light a fire to see something different." Another change leader also articulated that sometimes those hard conversations need to happen with himself. For him, this was an issue of integrity as he shared that he should work on changing himself before helping others learn to change themselves: "First, I think you have to be honest with yourself and understand that none of us like changing. You have to have that conversation with yourself first and I think if you have that understanding, the more you think about that, the more you reflect on that, the more empathetic you'll be to other people as you deliver that message of change." One change leader also mentioned that facilitating honest conversations was critical to change:

> I think it's getting them to name that they want change. I think a way to get towards change is to connect what we do with what we think. Bringing those two things together creates a fun disconnect to evaluate, which leaves room to change our minds if we notice that we're doing things that we actually don't believe in or we believe things and we're not doing them. Getting people to change is getting them to realize that we are disconnected in some way.

Moreover, change leaders invested a lot of time and energy developing and empowering others and themselves through relational means such as group book studies, staff leadership development, trainings, and assessments. Developing skills were important. In fact, a change leader said: "You have to be taught the skills." One change leader shared that she gives assessments called "inbox tests" in order to gather baseline information that she then uses to develop her employees. She said: "I think for our skills piece, we do what we call the inbox test. We do it every single year for every single employee. We do it to help us understand where they have gifts and where they might have opportunities for growth so that we know how to coach and train them." Another change leader also talked about equipping her clients who are victims of sexual violence: "And as they gain autonomy in their academic career is when we also build their leadership through leadership development, including facilitation skills, public speaking skills, and program design." Yet another change leader shared about how her organization teaches community leaders to change hygiene practices: "We've designed these really cool experiential learning programs for sanitation and hygiene, menstrual hygiene especially. So, every program that we run runs those learning experiences first." One change leader also said that equipping her clients well will help them develop skills for lifelong learning: "Giving them the tools for really long-term success and long-term change so they don't find themselves in similar situations again, I think is really key." Similarly, another change leader shared that he provides opportunities for learning and growth for his staff as a way to better serve their clients in their own journeys of change:

> If we are in the "business" of helping people reach their full potential, then we have to walk the walk. So, every team member has a personal development plan every year, which can include everything from running a 5K to finding a new mentor. This helps us when we interact with a client struggling to reach a learning goal

because we can empathize if we weren't able to accomplish some of our own goals as well. We want to make sure that we're walking the walk, which continues us on a path to learning, but then also gives us empathy for the folks we're serving and the path of learning they're on too.

Further, change leaders said it was critical to create a physically and psychologically safe environment in which people could learn and grow. They shared that this environment should be encouraging, affirming, and free from judgment so that people could be free to learn from mistakes or failure, and welcoming of transparent and honest conversations. In fact, a change leader said: "There has to be an encouragement to try again." Another change leader stated: "The only way you help each other grow is by trying to create a work environment where you're allowed to make mistakes, or mistakes are actually encouraged at times because that's how we grow." Similarly, one change leader said: "Being okay to change and being okay to fail needs to be part of the environment." Also, another change leader expressed: "It's a loving, caring environment that says we believe in you and we want you to believe in yourself and that you don't need to live like this. Life can be different and you can achieve your goals. And we're here to work with you to help you to do that." One change leader also shared: "I also think it's important for people to understand that you do have the ability to change, you have the ability to be transformative. You do have the ability to be someone different. And the time is now. It's right this moment. Now's when you start doing that." In particular, a change leader reiterated that a hopeful environment was necessary in the learning process. She shared: "I would say the primary element in change is hope. Without hope there is nothing to change for. Otherwise, why would we care to change or want to change or desire to change or do the hard work to change? So, I think it's instilling hope in the people you serve and the people you love." Specifically, for those who have experienced trauma, another change leader shared: "I think my job is really helping them notice that the light is already there and helping them look for that light so they can see it within themselves because the light's already there in them. It's not an external force. It's within them. Once they see that semblance of light, then they can start movement towards change." Another change leader who works to free girls from the sex industry underscored the importance of a safe environment for these girls who are learning to change:

The default for these girls becomes a brothel and the sex work. And for us, one of the great challenges is to try and help our girls see above and beyond that. How do we shape change—that is exceptionally difficult. But, what we do is we basically try and do it in a way where we are completely opposite of what they've experienced in that brothel on a daily basis. We're gracious. We're kind. We're forgiving. Our posture is one of humility and care, but still strength.

Similarly, another change leader reflected on the safe environment that she grew up in and her belief that "success in change and growth has to be paired with a high expectation and then a high level of support." One change leader also shared that a safe environment helps people open up and share information that might be critical to helping them learn to change. He said:

> If they can get to a place where they feel safe to really share it, I think that's the beginning. Then just walking with them in life. How you change somebody's life is you invest in them relationally and there's no way around that. I think if I'm going to help someone learn to change, I need to be someone really close to them in their life and I need to be someone they can really trust and love. And I also need to be able to present to them some humility that here's some things that are broken in my life that I'm working on. I think that's a big part of helping someone learn to change and for them to trust that you're struggling too.

Change leaders also mentioned that having models of growth and change was important to the learning process. For example, a change leader said that a model of growth and change is critical when he was trying to scale his organization: "But you can't just have an idea. It has to be anchored in something concrete because people are going to ask, 'What does it look like? How does it work?' You have to have a model and that's the thing that we've been building out." Likewise, another change leader said: "They felt like this is who I am, how it's always going to be. And unless they see someone like them who has gone through a transformation, they might not believe that they can too, you see. So, you have to hold up a model of what life could be." Relatedly, one change leader voiced: "I think a lot of times people have to see models. They have to see that something works." Moreover, yet another change leader gave similar wisdom on having models for those who do not know what other alternatives there could be:

> It's easy to say you want to learn and it's easy to say you want to change but those don't always actually mean what they mean. And what I think about often is fear. Fear of change drives a lot of people's decisions, or fear that this can't possibly be true or can't possibly be good. And I think about a community like ours where people have constantly been told they're not worth anything better, that really gets into one's psyche. And you believe that about

yourself. And so, I think first change comes with modeling what's actually possible.

Additionally, one change leader shared that his models came from the community in which he serves: "Speaking for myself, I learned how change happens from leaders in my community." He gave this example:

> There is a school that the city promised my community. The city promised us a school, but the city ended up backtracking and they withdrew it. Well, the families ended up doing a hunger strike. They didn't have resources. They didn't have connections. They didn't have the mayor's phone number or his ear, but they did a hunger strike for eleven days. They were getting attention from the media and eventually the city gave in and built a school in my community. That school is still there fifteen years later. How do you learn change? You learn it by watching the community and their persistence and the willingness to keep fighting even when it seems hopeless.

Plus, change leaders expressed that developing a plan for change and committing to that plan was helpful for those learning to change. For example, a change leader said: "How do I give them small steps so that they can accomplish the bigger thing? But then also, how do I help them see the bigger picture of what's going on?" In addition, another change leader talked about developing a plan this way: "I think you can work on one thing at a time with somebody. I feel like that's how God works with me." Moreover, another change leader shared that developing a plan for change should include small, attainable goals: "Making sure that you have attainable goals. I can say my vision is I want to lose one hundred pounds, but you need to have smaller goals, like losing five pounds this month, that meet up to that bigger vision." With a plan, change leaders said that commitment was required by all parties involved in the change or learning process. For example, a change leader shared:

> You have to commit to whatever that plan is, just as much as the other person has to commit to that plan. So now you're walking someone through that change. That again could take a long time because it takes a long time for people to change their habits or their thinking. It could take years to help somebody and then to stay on top of them and to provide resources and things like that.

Mutual commitment to a plan for change can be life-changing. One change leader shared that he has witnessed life change simply through the committed relationships of his volunteers and clients:

> When the client begins to realize that our volunteers are serving them completely altruistically, they begin to ask the question, "If you're willing to do that for me, what should I be willing to do for me?" When that happens, [makes blowing up motion with his hands and arms, then laughs] the whole program changes. That is when our program is at its very best.

Developing a plan for change also involved helping people remove barriers to change. For example, a change leader said: "We do everything we can to remove as many barriers as we can for someone to be able to succeed." Sometimes, removing barriers to change required creative solutions. One change leader shared a story about how he helped one of his employees learn to change through a creative solution that generated urgency for change:

> I have a team member here who was struggling with getting enough calls made to land enough sales and she wasn't hitting her goals. We kept meeting about it. I said, "All right, well what if we just paid your assistant an extra ten dollars every week whenever you got X many calls made?" And she said, "What's that going to do?" And I said, "You'll see what it does." And immediately everything turned around for her because the assistant was creating urgency for her on a regular basis to get that extra ten bucks. I think that's a piece of this where we need to build creative, innovative mechanisms that help somebody resolve things and see that it is urgent to change.

In summary, continuing momentum for a desired change had four themes: seek teamwork, surrender control, shape cultural practices within organization, and steward care and development of others. As cited by the majority of change leaders, intentionally building a team with the right people was important to these change agent leaders as a way to continue momentum for change through collective impact. Teams included the right hires, community partners, the people they served, friends, family, and the next generation of leaders as some of the most influential connection points that broadened the ripples of change. Change leaders also frequently mentioned that change cannot be controlled and many of their ultimate goals were to work themselves out of a job. These insights were given with the awareness and hope that change should not and does not ultimately depend on their leadership, but rather, that they are only a piece of the larger change puzzle already in motion in the world. Moreover, change leaders focused attention on the need to anchor change within their organization by shaping cultural practices that would remind others of new habits and processes, encourage staff to live out cultural values, and shift thinking around fundraising. Last, change leaders invested significant time and energy toward caring for and developing others as they helped people learn to change.

Change leaders stressed the importance of being self-motivated to change, of being aware of the problems and issues that need changing, of developing skills for continued change, of creating a safe environment where learning could occur, of providing models for change, of facilitating hard, honest, and uncomfortable conversations, and of formulating and committing to a plan for change. These were the necessary ingredients to helping others learn to change that would influence the staying power of change over time.

Chapter 7

The People, Process, and Purpose of Change

As an Asian–American, specifically Korean American, woman who spent most of my childhood and all of my adolescent years being raised in Salt Lake City, Utah, and now leading in very multicultural spaces as an adult, I constantly navigate the ebb and flow of my intersectional identities (Crenshaw 1989). This means that different parts of who I am contribute to both my privileges and oppressions in the spaces I occupy. This also means that different parts of who I am work together in the ultimate expression of my unique gifts and the beauty of who I am regardless of the space I occupy. As I move through diverse terrain, I have learned that change leadership requires and often demands integration of parts to form an ultimate more beautiful expression of the whole. Similar to the work that goes into embracing all of who we are individually, it is hard work to embrace the beauty that exists in everyone else, even those who resist change. Leading change often requires healthy integration of the people, the process, and the purpose to generate outcomes that lead to flourishing. Hopefully, this chapter illuminates a way forward that brings us more together than apart.

The previous four chapters described the primary themes that emerged from my research of the relational communication strategies of change agents in non-profit organizations. Four themes emerged under the first research question: *In relationship with others, how do non-profit change agents catalyze a sense of urgency for a desired change?* The four themes were placed within a larger context of two beliefs commonly held by all participants: (1) change is possible; and (2) change is already in motion. Chapter 3 is dedicated to the theme of discerning the change landscape due to its overwhelming strength as a data point. Discerning the change landscape involved the need for change agents to (a) discern their capabilities and capacity, and in general, to grow in self-awareness; and (b) discern the contextually nuanced layers of change in order to understand when, where, and how to catalyze change. Chapter 4 summarizes the remaining themes of developing relationships of trust, disrupting the current narrative, and designing organizations for change.

DOI: 10.4324/9781003272243-8

Likewise, four themes emerged under the second research question: *In relationship with others, how do non-profit change agents connect people toward a desired change?* and are captured in Chapter 5. Themes include: (1) cultivating multivocality by creating multiple channels for communication, dialogue, and feedback loops; (2) co-constructing relational bridges with the people they served as well as with organizational partners through relationships that were mutually transformative; (3) centering community-driven dreams by listening to the needs and dreams of community members and working to see those fulfilled; and (4) creating avenues for inspiration by affirming and encouraging the people they served as well as celebrating the accomplishment of achieved change-related goals.

Finally, we covered the four themes that emerged under research question three: *In relationship with others, how do non-profit change agents continue momentum for a desired change?* Chapter 6 walks through the following themes: (1) seeking teamwork in order to continue momentum for a desired change; (2) surrendering control by constantly collaborating with other change agents in their communities as well as recognizing that they are ultimately not in full control of change; (3) shaping cultural practices within their organizations that helped continue momentum for a desired change. Cultural practices included keeping integrity to their organizational values, inquiring about and receiving feedback from others, integrating work and family life in a healthy way, and shaping a philosophy of fundraising; and (4) stewarding the care and development of others around them, particularly in the context of helping others learn to change. Change leaders mentioned that helping others learn to change required a learning posture and self-motivation from the people seeking change. Helping others learn to change also involved (a) hard, honest, and uncomfortable conversations; (b) empowerment or professional development of all involved in the learning cycle; (c) a physically and psychologically safe environment; (d) models of growth and change others can emulate or be inspired by; and (e) developing and committing to a plan for change.

This chapter will discuss how the research findings can complement and integrate with current theories and practices of change agents in non-profit organizations. I argue that change agents can catalyze the need for, connect people toward, and sustain momentum for change best when they use relational communication strategies to influence key stakeholders in the direction of a change mission. The primary interest underlying the current study is the trifold intersection of relationships, communication, and change. The topics of relationships, communication, and change can be understood as three dimensions that interact with one another as well as with the change agent. These three dimensions are neither in competition

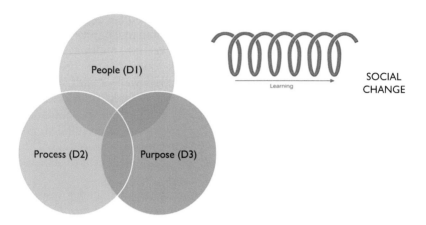

Figure 7.1 Three Dimensions of Leading Change Well.

nor in conflict, but rather, simultaneously work together or against the successful movement toward a change mission.

Because of their interaction, I will also integrate models found in each respective topic area to build my argument. I have chosen to use the language of people, process, and purpose to represent the three dimensions of relationships, communication, and change. This new language will both outline and facilitate the discussion for this chapter. Therefore, the road map for my argument can be imagined as a dialogue between the change agent and (Dimension 1: People)—his or her relationship with people involved in the change process; (Dimension 2: Process)—how and what they communicate to one another; and (Dimension 3: Purpose)—the change mission itself. I believe this integrative method best represents the change agents in my study who sought to first discern the change already taking place around them so they could build change initiatives together with others rather than advocating for a new change initiative on their own (Figure 7.1).

Dimension 1: People—Relationships for Change

"We will be able to progress at the speed of trust" (Change Leader). This change leader named what all change leaders in this study shared—a genuine desire to develop trust with people before change is introduced, as well as the desire to deepen trust along the way in order to move change forward. When discussing relationships for change, it is important to first address the change agent leader's perspective about and posture toward people. This will be discussed below through the lens of humility and humble leadership as one way participants developed trusting relationships with others.

The word humility itself comes from the Latin *humus*, meaning "earth," and *humilis*, meaning "on the ground" (per the Online Etymology Dictionary, accessed in 2019).

Therefore, humble leadership can be characterized as "leadership from the ground" or "bottom up leadership" (Owens and Hekman 2012, 787). This reveals that even though change agents can hold executive-level positions in their organizations, they have the rare ability to lead others through personal connection by integrating seamlessly on the ground. Humble leadership is critical to change agency because it "will create and reflect the relationships that can respond to this accelerating rate of systemic change and will empower workgroups to build and maintain critical adaptive capacity to capitalize on accelerating change" (Schein 2018, 6). Although different kinds of relationship building and maintaining occur at all points of a change cycle, it is imperative that we focus on building relationships of *trust* at the beginning of the change cycle. Here, change agents seek to earn the trust of others by being a consistent presence who asks questions out of genuine curiosity, listens well, and acts with integrity.

Several theories on trust are based on social exchange theory, suggesting that "trust forms through repeated exchange of interests between two entities, or through the interaction of people's values, attitudes, and emotions" (Liu and Wang 2013, 231; Jones and George 1998). Similarly, Komives et al. argue that collaborative efforts are built through trust, which takes intentional investment and attention over time (2017). They write, "Trust does not happen immediately or automatically; it must be cultivated. When groups come together for the first time, people bring their own agendas, values, perceptions, motivations, and histories. Building trust and openness takes time and commitment" (Komives et al. 2017, 116). Although building trust takes effort and risk, trust can be "contagious" (Kouzes and Posner 2012, 222), thereby influencing quicker catalysis and eventual diffusion of change.

We also see how the discerning change agent interacts with the people dimension of change. With humility, participants who discerned their own strengths and weaknesses were better able to develop trusting relationships both inside and outside their organizations. Their self-awareness helped them wisely navigate their place within the complexity of collective social change. Without self-awareness, change agents are unlikely to know whom to invite, how to invite them, and to know at which points in the change cycle would be both accessible and strategic for others to engage. Although growth in self-awareness is a lifelong journey, it is necessary for change agents to seek intentional growth in their self-awareness before driving change initiatives. This way, the seeds of change can come forth from a healthy internal state of mind and then externally take root in life-giving ways.

Another way non-profit change agents prioritized relationship building to accomplish a change mission was catalyzing a sense of urgency for change by designing their organizations with open systems. Open systems built social capital by giving opportunity and access for people on the inside of their organizations to interact with those on the outside, and vice versa. These inside-outside interactions often blurred the lines of division and hierarchy that characterize more closed systems. Participants also reported blurred lines between the work of change that took place inside their organizations versus outside. The reason for this is that change often took place as a result of listening to the feedback of the people they serve, and then seeking to develop trust with them by acting on their feedback. As reflected in participant reporting, intentionally asking for and receiving feedback was a significant piece of the continuous process of discernment and learning. Participants desired feedback from diverse stakeholders with a genuine desire for collaboration and collective action. Feedback determined the direction of change as well as informed how the organization itself should pivot to better accomplish a change mission. Change agents developed deeper trust with stakeholders when they acted upon feedback rather than simply listening to it. Although the act of listening to feedback was critical, action catalyzed from a feedback partnership built credibility and trust with people who had experienced change failure. Feedback loops also created a level of continuous accountability to the people change agents sought to serve.

Participants invited others into relationships with genuine curiosity to understand different perspectives and narratives. As reported, they approached relationship building through inquiry, listening, and committing to people over time through action. The depth of trust depended on the degree of action taken based upon feedback or stories exchanged. Therefore, the act of listening or a posture of genuine curiosity did not by themselves deepen trust, especially with those being served. Regardless of the size or type of change cycle, change agents must recognize the importance of completing cycles of change to the subsequent construction of their integrity and trustworthiness as a change agent. For this reason, commitment to change over time that includes care for people along the way becomes a critical factor of change success.

With an openness to being shaped by and for others, the change agents in this study led organizations that facilitated collective change-making. The design of their organizations reflected participants' personal ways of interacting with others, which, as previously mentioned, were often characterized by a posture of humility and learning. Due to their high value for learning, the open design of their organizations provided the optimal conditions not only to incubate change but also for the organization itself to change—both of which require considerable and continuous learning. This can be described as a social learning process constructed through a social and relational network of people and organizations. Westoby and Lyons argue that this "social network creates the crucial container that *enables* people to shift their perceptions and take the risk of collective organizing and social action" (2017, 228). This social framing of learning helps make sense of the type of learning that takes place in order to build a foundation of trust that can propel collective change.

Consistent with the character of change agents in this study, it is important to mention that there continues to be a strong others-centered focus as the change journey moves toward increasing empowerment and facilitation of agency (Kotter 2021). This movement was important to participants because they did not want to create a culture of change dependency or change drift by stakeholders riding on the coattails of a change initiative. They desired stakeholders to take ownership over change and to join them as co-creators of a bigger movement. In fact, Komives, Wagner and Associates (2017) state that partnerships create momentum for greater collective social impact. For this reason, participants remarked that relational bridge building was a co-constructed endeavor and took relationships beyond the initial development of trust that was needed to introduce change itself. Co-construction involved a different dimension of trust characterized by shared power and faith in new partners to work collectively in the difficult tensions of social change complexity. Some scholars refer to this kind of leadership as "boundary-spanning collaboration" (Ospina and Foldy 2010, 292; Gasson and Elrod 2006) because organizational boundaries are crossed in order to foster collective action (see Figure 7.5). Ospina and Foldy also state, "Collective action is, therefore, essential but it cannot happen without first connecting across differences. Bridging differences within a complex web of interconnected yet separate actors is not easy. Yet the potential for connectedness is always present in human beings" (2010, 292). We can say that the nonprofit change agents in this study exhibit the use of systems thinking, which is the "the ability to understand interconnections in such a way as to achieve a *desired* purpose" (Stroh 2015, 16).

In their relentless work to create and understand interconnections, change agents also understood that there is a relationship among problems as well. For this reason, they sought to build relational bridges on as many levels and through as many spheres of influence as possible with the knowledge that improving relationships could optimize the whole (Stroh 2015). In addition, change agents included themselves in the diagnosis of the social problems they sought to solve. They recognized their potential for harm by their lack of awareness, lack of care, or unchecked pride. This way of thinking is also congruent with systems thinking research that argues that we create our own problems (Stroh 2015) and thereby contribute to the complexity and wickedness that characterize social issues. However, change agents did not hesitate to learn from their own mistakes, resulting in wisdom and advice offered to emerging non-profit change agent leaders (see Chapter 9).

In summary, it was of utmost importance to change agents that they lived out their personal and organizational values, which highlighted their desire to live a life of integrity and cohesion. Since all change agents in this study valued both relationships and communication, I will underscore that change agents consistently looked for ways to create and sustain multi-layered and multi-dimensional interconnections to leverage them toward a desired social change. They sought interconnections not only in their personal lives, but also as a regular mode of operating through the work of social change. Without the desire for interconnections or the skill to facilitate them, the work of social change cannot possibly be as impactful.

Dimension 2: Process—Communicating for Change

"Relationships and conversations are inseparable and influence each other. The manner of engagement—the way we develop a relationship with another person—influences the kind and quality of conversations that we can have with each other, and likewise the conversations we begin to have with each other will influence the kind and quality of our relationships" (Anderson 2012, 14). When communicative processes and people are deeply intertwined, it is easy to imagine the repercussions of one destructive person in the mix. On the flip side, we can also imagine the positive change that can result when people and processes intermingle for the good of one another.

Communication that influences people to accomplish change together is critical to successful change diffusion. The purpose of communication is to learn potential for collective change through newly built connections. Communicating with this purpose assumes that every person has the agency, or some power, to participate in a movement for change. While not every person might lead the change mission, every person can still become a partner who helps accomplish the change mission. Based on reflections from the change agents in this study, communication that is relationally focused moves people from a present state of collective change potential to a future state of collective change agency. Rather than seeking to empty or rid the world of its problems, change agents intentionally communicate with others to construct a world full of relationships that emanate respect and dignity.

It should be noted that communication strategies vary by context as well as by the personality of the change agent. However, both the desire for change and the process by which change agents seek to execute change are shaped by their lived value for human respect and dignity.

With words being one of the primary ways human beings show respect and dignity to one another, it makes sense that the communication strategies used to diffuse change become of utmost importance to the failure or success of a change mission. When change agents diffuse change, they also encounter people who need to learn or unlearn specific ways of thinking or behaving. Such encounters challenge change agents to communicate with others so that they understand new learning and can apply it in their context.

As noted previously, change agents in this study reported that their work often takes place under the radar and behind the scenes. Being under the radar meant that change agents not only sought seamless integration alongside their partners, but also did not seek the hero spotlight. The literature places hero leadership in the individual realm, where the focus is on a single person's behavior or personality so that the individual leader receives credit for success (Zulu 2015). However, it is clear in this study that non-profit change agents' preferred mode of operation was to center and highlight the people they served within their respective contexts. By doing so, change agents respected the autonomy and dignity of the people they served while also recognizing that change agents do not hold secret solutions to the problems they seek to solve. In this regard, connecting others to a desired change rests in the ability of non-profit change agents to draw out the needs and dreams of the people they serve through dialogic spaces.

Centering voices that are often overlooked took precedence for non-profit change agents desiring to connect people toward a desired change. Often, the act of centering new voices took place by convening dialogue with diverse stakeholders around a table (sometimes physical tables, but oftentimes just psychologically safe spaces primed for conversation) and creating enough psychological safety to draw out stories that regularly revealed hurts, needs, dreams, motivations, and passions. Edmonson's research suggests that creating psychological safety is critical to the social change process because of its influence to engender social learning. For example, Edmonson (1999, 2004) states that the three major antecedents to psychological safety are trust, positive relations, and familiarity. With trust developed at the beginning of the change cycle, the hoped-for progression toward dialogue is an open exchange of thoughts, experiences, feelings, uncertainties, and/or lack of understanding (Howorth, Smith, and Parkinson 2012).

As mentioned in the literature review, dialogue creates space for people to connect to the change process by providing opportunities for diverse voices to speak toward the co-creation of the social change that will directly affect their communities (Kuenkel 2016). Primarily convened by the change agents themselves, or at least ideated by some of them with execution by external facilitators, dialogue was not only directed by the voices of others, but also convened to receive human interaction with strategic goals with the desire to be fully transparent in moments of decision-making. Further, dialogue was convened to ensure consistency in shared language and understanding surrounding the reason why decisions were being made. As such, dialogue was seen as a participatory process to include and involve others, thereby affirming the strong value that non-profit change agents had for collective action rather than simple transactions. As Dutta underscores, moving toward action is especially important for people who normally live in the margins of society without the privilege of normally participating in dialogue (Dutta 2011). It is encouraging that the non-profit change agents in this study worked toward social change with full awareness that their trustworthiness and integrity were on the line without action that showed their commitment to add value (see Figure 7.2).

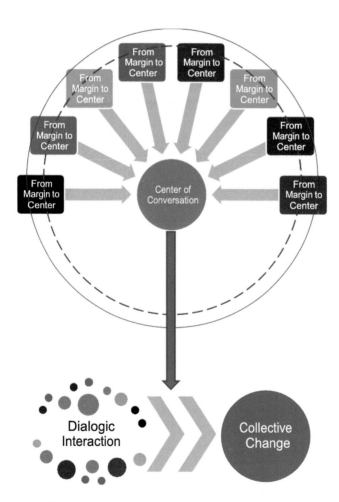

Figure 7.2 Open Dialogue & Collective Action.

Moreover, mirroring the open concept design of the non-profit organizations included in this study, non-profit change agents convened dialogic spaces as open concepts as well.

Therefore, they did not necessarily facilitate dialogue with specific rules of engagement, but they took cues from the dialogue participants themselves, especially with regards to the direction of the dialogue, even if a specific topic was placed on the dialogue table. However, because of their deeply ingrained value for respect, human dignity/agency, and suspending judgment, non-profit change agents naturally engaged the dialogic rules of engagement prominent in the literature without explicitly setting those ground rules (Isaacs 1999; Yankelovich 1999; Freire 2000; Buber 2002; Colwill 2015).

In dialogue with others, it was essential to the non-profit change agents in this study that they connected people to a desired change by communicating vision, mission, hope, affirmation, and encouragement with intentionally positive language. As reported, inspiring all engaged stakeholders by connecting the desired change to human emotions proved to strengthen commitment to and ownership of a change process. This continues to affirm that the change process is a very human experience that, when leveraged wisely with the intent for common good, has potential for collective impact that can ripple deep and wide. In fact, Seyranian states that "communication may be a key mechanism for change-oriented leaders," especially when "emotional significance" is attached to a person's "membership" in a group or collective (2014, 468–69). In order to connect people to a desired change, it is important to keep in mind the significant influence of shared group identity as a means of motivation. In addition, this is also a challenge to all non-profit change agents to steer clear of manipulating people's emotions so as to not unnecessarily create more harm than good for communities already experiencing systemic inequity and division.

The change agents in this study also communicated for change by disrupting the current narrative as a way to strengthen relationships. Change agents revealed that disruption of the current narrative meant verbally naming unhealthy and/or toxic disconnection or conflict between people and systems. With the value for human dignity, disruption was done carefully but also with conviction and courage to catalyze the urgency for a desired change. In their discernment of social fragmentation in the current narrative of their surroundings, participants remarked that it was critical to bring people together in conversation to talk through the often uncomfortable and difficult issues that kept relational integration and collective action at bay. As reported, participants used radical candor to create a stronger collective social fabric. These conversations happened both inside their organizations as part of their intentionally designed organizational cultures and outside their organizations with stakeholders in acts of perspective-taking or learning across differences. Although some conversations were uncomfortable, change agents found it necessary to engage in them for the sake of those they serve. Contrary to assumed opinion, radical candor happens best in caring environments (Scott 2017). It is important to point out that change agents valued caring for people along the change journey rather than demanding or forcing change upon them. They were fully aware that the language shared with others and the relational capital they built shaped the direction of change toward failure or success.

Strengthening relational capital happened through shared language as well as developing shared social change goals. As a result, all stakeholders become connected to the desired change in a new way. Such collaboration involved conversation to bring others into the change journey and to draw out the strengths of each party. This way, the multiplication of strengths can lead to a combined effect of change that ripples further than could be possible without the invitation to others to collaborate. Collaborating with other identified change agents created opportunities to learn together, which is one of the best ways to develop trusting relationships through direct feedback (Edmonson 2012; Schein 2018). As referenced earlier, the literature also defines this as collaborative transformative learning where relationships and the conversations that take place within them are the means through which learning takes place (Fisher-Yoshida, Geller, and Schapiro 2009). Affirming the findings in this research, Rogers states, "Social learning and the diffusion of innovation have much in common: Both theories seek to explain how individuals change their overt behavior as a result of communication with other individuals" (2003, 342).

Communicating for change also expressed itself through the cultural practices that change agents shaped within their organizations. Cultural practices acted as reminders toward a new way of being and being together. However, these newly cultivated practices tended to compete with old ones that people had often unconsciously adopted, and thus were not even aware of. Change agents then worked to dismantle the old by consistently communicating and pointing people toward the new. The act of dismantling the old was critical because the old culture can ultimately overcome and dismantle the new culture trying to take root. Typically, in organizations with deeply ingrained old cultural practices, communication is often lacking because there is no need to communicate anything new. The act of dismantling is also a complex issue both inside and outside the organization that only adds to the complexity of social change. Dismantling can create anxiety or chaos within an organization that the change agent must then also manage. However, change agents discerned shifts toward the adoption of new cultural practices when both internal and external stakeholders began to articulate new organizational values.

Some change agents also sought to receive feedback from stakeholders located outside the organization regarding the organization's ability to express new cultural values. Receiving this feedback from others provided perspective to know which values and practices needed more anchoring.

This section would not be complete without the acknowledgment of the Christian change agents in this study, who often mentioned their relationship with God and their desire to consistently communicate with God about their work. These change agents believed that God was in control, and therefore, their human tendencies to seek control were acts of futility. In addition, they believed that God could grow or stop the social change movement at any time based on God's good and loving plan for the world and those God created to inhabit it. Moreover, Christian change agents found renewed strength and life in God as they sought God for refuge and healing from the challenges of social change work. Conversing with God through prayer was a means through which Christian change agents gained perspective, provision, wisdom, and joy as they surrendered control to the one who they believed had called them to the work of social change in the first place.

Dimension 3: Purpose—The Change Mission

"We need to be able to pivot to move forward without compromising the overall mission and values of the organization" (Change Leader). The third dimension in leading change well is the ability of the change agent to discern both the change already taking place in a particular context and the changes required to continue momentum forward. All this without losing perspective of the guiding mission, or North Star, of the organization. Participants did their due diligence in collecting data and research as part of the discernment process before change was introduced.

Subsequently, data collection informed their strategic plans for change. Even with very capable strategic plans, participants often shifted into emergent processes that allowed for the deeper iteration and learning needed to approach complex social change problems through innovation (discussed later in this chapter). Also, participants often mentioned that as a result of social change complexity, they could not possibly fully understand the solutions to the wicked problems they sought to solve. Having this awareness was consistent with the humble posture that accompanied awareness of their own limitations.

Their reporting is well aligned with Buono's model where he differentiates change management processes as "directed change, planned change or iterative changing" (Buono and Kerber 2018, 1), the use of which are dependent upon the interaction between business complexity and socio-technical uncertainty. He argues that as complexity and uncertainty increase, change agents need to know when and how to shift between planned and guided changing processes. Each process also requires different ways of relating to and communicating with others. As described, the non-profit change agents in this study had the agility to shift seamlessly between planned and iterative changing processes and were often comfortable with living in the tension of the space where these processes converge.

The third dimension also intimately interacts with relationships and communication. In fact, participants often mentioned that collaborative partnerships were developed with other organizations that seemed aligned with the mission and values of their organizations. Further, participants constantly communicated their mission and values in relationships with others to catalyze, connect, and continue momentum for change. Therefore, the purpose of social change was *for* people, accomplished *with* people, and communicated often *to* people.

The social change mission remained steady while the combination of various cycles of innovation to accomplish a change mission iterated. It is important to note here that the regeneration of a social innovation cycle does not mean that the current cycle has ended. By contrast, since this study focuses on change success, the regeneration of an innovation cycle can be described as the integration of continuing the current cycle and beginning another iteration through innovation. This is not a surprise since all of the non-profit change agents in this study self-identified as social entrepreneurs. To non-profit change agents, continuing momentum for a change mission included an investment in the future of their organizations in ways that would once again catalyze innovation and creativity. As mentioned previously, in designing their organizations as places of constant learning, change agents set the stage for innovative capacity from the beginning. In fact, research suggests, "Leaders can create and manage an organizational culture that promotes innovation, can be product champions or heroic innovators who support innovation throughout the process of its implementation, and can create organizational structure needed to support innovativeness" (Jaskyte 2004, 154; Peters and Waterman 1982). Visually, Figure 7.3 captures this illustration and is adapted from Everett Rogers (2003).

Continuing momentum for a desired change mission was consistently placed in the context of surrendering control over the change process. Surrendering control was mentioned when participants were asked to imagine ten to fifteen years out from the time of the interview to tell me what they would do to sustain a movement of change over time. Surrendering control is both a posture and an act. It is a posture because change agents recognized that social change is an uncontrollable phenomenon that takes a long time. Therefore, they engaged social change with a long-term perspective that continued to grow their humility as well as helped influence the pace of their work in relation to their personal lives.

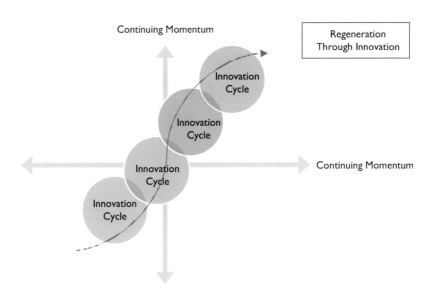

Figure 7.3 Cycles of Innovation.
Source: (adapted from Everett Rogers 2003).

In short, change agents sought to live as whole persons with their work for social change characterized by an ebb and flow and a keen awareness that the burden of social change did not rest solely on their shoulders.

In addition, the act of surrendering is exactly that—intentional actions that hand off the work of social change to others who will carry the baton into the future. Plastrik, Taylor, and Cleveland (2014) write, "a network can provide an adaptive and sustainable capacity … something no other organizing method can fully achieve" (29). As such, the work of social change becomes a beautiful visual of a continuous relay race where the change baton switches from one runner to the next. However, since social change is not solely dependent on individual change agent actors detached from social change institutions or communities, when the baton is dropped, it can safely land into the net of the social change network. Faust et al. write, "A network perspective on organizations emphasizes the relational links between them alongside the attributes of particular organizations" (Faust et al. 2015, 126). This can only occur, however, if change agents work toward creating this network through relational communication strategies that strengthen it.

Surrendering control involves strengthening the social change network because social change requires the collaborative efforts of the collective team. Change agents considered their teams to include the right hires,

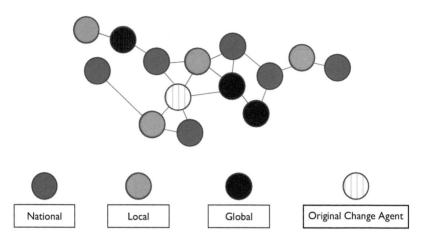

Figure 7.4 Continuing Change Mission Via Social Change Network.

friends, community partners, board members, funders, and emerging change agent leaders, to name a few. Each team member contributed to the social change mission, either through official professional partnerships or through unofficial yet equally important support from family or friends. Through the collective, the social change mission continues to ripple through the momentum created by strategically connecting local, national, or global agents of change, with each connection including both individuals and institutions (see Figure 7.4). For the sake of the social problems they sought to solve, but even more so for the people who are caught in the harmful web of social issues, change agents were aware that growth and scale could not occur if they held a tight grip over change.

Loosening their grip over change breathed new life into the work toward a change mission because new connections brought new energy and perspectives that confronted change agents' own blind spots. It is significant to note that the change agents in this study truly perceived others as collaborators rather than competitors and also believed in their collaborators' expertise to benefit the whole. Research on collaboration in the non-profit social change sector also states, "Individual organizations may be effective or ineffective at achieving narrower organizational goals, but network dynamics including collaborations, referrals, and information exchanges between organizations can play a key role in systems' ability to provide holistic service and effective community interventions" (Faust et al. 2015, 126). The reason why communication is critical, however, is that "a network's communication infrastructure is essential to the network's success because it will enable or impede collaboration" (Plastrik, Taylor, and Cleveland 2014, 58).

A unique benefit of teamwork is the opportunity for others to keep change agents accountable to learning, to their mission, and even to resting. Their desire for accountability once again revealed their humility along with their awareness that they cannot do the work of social change alone. The leadership literature defines accountability as "an implicit or explicit expectation that one may be called on to justify one's actions to others, which tends to motivate reflection on one's own decisions and behaviors" (Giessner et al. 2013, 659; Tetlock 1992; De Dreu, Nijstad, and van Knippenberg 2008). Accountability was critical to continuing momentum for a social change mission because not only were change agents able to keep others accountable to change, but others kept change agents accountable to working toward the big-picture social change mission, as well as the learning and intermittent rest needed to progressively move forward.

To change agents, consistency mattered as they looked ahead and thought through how to continue momentum toward a desired social change mission when social change itself is so unpredictable and uncontrollable. While still remaining agile in their organizational design, change agents sought to create stability through cultivating organizational values that would act as anchors to keep the purpose and vision for change in front of people. Change agents hoped that anchors would remind others of the new behavior required to live into the change they were working toward. This hope was also connected to change agents' desire for integrity in their work and to hire the best fit for their organizations (to be discussed below). Change agents also understood the concept of sustainability more as support rather than equating the concept of sustainability with building indestructible self-made empires. To change agents, providing anchors of support for the change itself, as well as providing social capital support for the people affected by change, was the most effective means to fully realize the social change mission.

In their work to accomplish a social change mission, change agents often communicated that change was also required of them. They mentioned that while leading change, the change agent should not separate him- or herself from the possibility of being changed. By doing so, the change agent remains too detached from the realities of a change process, thereby increasing the chances of leading change harmfully rather than empathically. There needs to be a simultaneous transformation that takes place in the life of the change agent, the physical places, or communities in which change agents seek to implement change, and in the lives of those being influenced by the change agent. Mutual growth and learning in all areas are signposts of collective change success directed at the common good of all involved and multiply the strength of the healthy relationships and communicative processes needed to continue momentum for change. Drilling

Figure 7.5 Cultivating an Environment of Learning to Change.

down, change agents identified eight pillars that help people learn to change, with the ideal situation involving all eight pillars interacting simultaneously (see Figure 7.5).

Moving clockwise, change agents were adamant that learning to change required self-motivation. Without self-motivation, learning to change can be difficult due to the inability to force genuine transformation. Within the context of change, it is appropriate to think of motivation as self-efficacy because of its identification with various change theories (Chirila and Constantin 2016). According to social cognitive theory, a person with high self-efficacy "might initiate and maintain behavior change with less difficulty than a person low in self-efficacy" (Chirila and Constantin 2016, 21; Bandura 1997). As such, a person with high self-efficacy most likely has a posture that is open and ready for change. Change agents mentioned that if people did not already have this posture, they could create an environment to restore their belief that change is possible.

Having honest conversations was uncomfortable for all involved, including the change agents themselves, but they believed in the power of communication to bridge interrelationships. Because this is very much aligned with change agents' own value for self-awareness, it is not surprising that they facilitated honest conversations to bring problems to the table as a way to bring attention to relational dysfunction for the sake of growth. Self-awareness is critical to change because "self-awareness involves knowing how your values, beliefs, assumptions, attitudes and preferences affect your behavior" (Levasseur 1991, 131). Change agents often facilitated conversations that required talking through both individual and relational problems, some of which needed to be brought to people's consciousness due to lack of awareness. Proximity through honest conversations draws out emotions that not only reveal the brokenness of the world, but also the darkness that resides within oneself. This can be quite disarming and unpleasant, but growing in self-awareness both internally and externally in our relationships with others is essential to the work of change, with social value maximization happening through collaborative efforts (Chang et al. 2016).

Also connected to the theme of continuous learning, change agents mentioned that it was important to equip others as well as themselves for both current and future change through skill-building opportunities. Buckwalter (2014) also notes that professional support and empowerment is vital to others' own positive evaluation of their impact toward a cause. Unique to this study, change agents suggested that skill-building opportunities take place within relational contexts in community with others. Learning new skills with a community of people set people up for future success and change agility, which is an important capacity especially when involved in complex organizations such as non-profit social change institutions. Becoming agile means that change becomes normal in one's understanding and acceptance of continual improvement and progress that result from lifelong learning (Worley, Williams, and Lawler 2014). Regardless of one's stakeholder position, change agility is necessary for any future collaboration needed for continued innovation and growth (Shuman and Twombly 2010).

According to change agents, the ideal environment to inspire and cultivate change is characterized by a place that is both physically and psychologically safe to take risks and make mistakes. Change agents mentioned that physical safety was an additional necessity for those who had endured trauma to their bodies. For this reason, the convener of a learning environment becomes a critical person in the change process, not only to be a physically safe person, but also to be someone who can ably hold the tensions within the field of conversation for all involved (Isaacs 1999). Psychological safety was important to create a positive climate for learning, a climate characterized by "warm and authentic relationships with others, access to trusted peers to scaffold and validate learning, and opportunities to take risks and make mistakes without ridicule" (Wanless and Winters 2018, 41). Moreover, psychological safety "is the feeling that you can tolerate—and even feel comfortable with—an inherently uncomfortable situation" (Wanless and Winters 2018, 42). By creating environments that are psychologically safe, change agents were able to work collaboratively with others through the exchange of diverse opinions, open questions, and creative solutions to individual or social problems (Edmonson and Roloff 2009)—all necessary ingredients to deep and meaningful learning.

In their work to help people learn to change, change agents realized that it is helpful to present models of change to show others that change is possible. This is connected to motivating and inspiring others to change, but what underlies modeling is a hopeful facilitation of the change process. Despite the challenges faced by change agents in this study, they continued to display unwavering hope in others, in themselves, and in their combined participation in the change process as a whole. Helland and Winston (2005) define hope as "an activating force that enables people, even when faced with the most overwhelming obstacles, to envision a promising future and to set and pursue goals" (43). Helland and Winston also state that hope arises in relational contexts and can lead to more conversations about the action needed to reach change goals with others (2005).

Relatedly, translating the above conversations by developing a plan for change with mutual commitment from everyone involved in the change process was critical for the change leaders. Developing a plan that is "designed to be a living, breathing document, that co-creates a narrative that is both strategic and relational" is necessary (Brosan and Levin 2017, 67). In addition, commitment to change is significant because the literature states that change agents often underestimate the attitudes of their stakeholders with regards to change (Armenakis, Harris, and Mossholder 1993; Bartunek et al. 2006; Van der Voet, Kuipers, and Groeneveld 2015). Plans for change that included both short-term and long-term goals are necessary to give a sense of big-perspective vision and immediate tangible achievement. Although some plans for change were individualized based on a person's needs, the plans still required commitment from change agents as well as others involved in the change process to provide accountability, encouragement, discernment, and care along the way. This is important because the research recognizes that the interaction of self-efficacy and collective identity at the group level contribute to change commitment (Ling, Guo, and Chen 2018). In their collaborative efforts, reciprocal transformation often took place, which, again, is a fruit of change success.

Walking with people through the learning that takes place throughout a change initiative was a role that change agents took seriously because of their respect and love for others. We can see that building relationships continues to be a thread here, but expresses itself as investment in the future of others. Change agents not only understood change to be connected to social learning, as mentioned previously, but also to individual learning. Change agents were fully aware that working with and for others took tremendous time, energy, and investment that needed to be bolstered by both care and developmental learning opportunities for themselves and others.

In summary, this discussion has revealed that successful change agency begins and continues with discerning change agents who prioritize and leverage the generative interaction of communication and relationships throughout the work of realizing a social change mission. Contrary to the reputation that change agents might have as deviants who thoughtlessly cause harm to organizations through change failure, this study shows that true change agents are careful and wise in their approach to change. This is not an easy skill to master, however, given the need for change agents to facilitate interrelationships across diverse stakeholders both inside and outside their organizations, all the while working on a spectrum of activities that take them from big-picture thinking to on-the-ground service in a matter of hours. Change agents in this study have provided tangible relational communication strategies to consider for those interested in pursuing change in their sphere of influence.

References

Anderson, Harlene. 2012. "Collaborative Relationships and Dialogic Conversations: Ideas for a Relationally Responsive Practice." *Family Process* 51, no. 1: 8–24.

Armenakis, A.A., Harris, S.G., and Mossholder, K.W. 1993. "Creating Readiness for Organizational Change." *Human Relations* 46: 681–703.

Bandura, A. 1997. *Self-Efficacy: The Exercise of Control.* New York: W.H. Freeman.

Bartunek J.M., Rousseau D.M., Rudolph J.W., and DePalma, J.A. 2006. "On the Receiving End: Sensemaking, Emotion and Assessments of an Organizational Change Initiated by Others." *The Journal of Applied Behavioral Science* 42: 182–206.

Brosan, Debra and Levin, Michele. 2017. "Strategic Planning in the Nonprofit World. What Does It Look Like?" *Practicing OD* 49, no. 4: 67–69.

Buber, Martin. 2002. *Between Man and Man.* Translated by Ronald Gregor-Smith. London, New York: Routledge.

Buckwalter, N.D. 2014. "The Potential for Public Empowerment through Government Organized Participation." *Public Administration Review* 74, no. 5: 573–584.

Buono, Tony and Kerber, Kenneth. 2018. "In Defense of Directed Change: A Viable Approach in the Rhythm of Change." *ResearchGate.* Paper presented at the Management Consulting Division, Academy of Management Annual Meeting, August 13, 2018.

Chang, Jung-Nung, Seetoo, Dah-Hsian, Yu, Chwo-Ming, and Cheng, Chia-Yi. 2016. "Relational Management Mechanisms for Strategic Alliances among Nonprofit Organizations." *International Journal of Voluntary and Nonprofit Organizations* 27, no. 5: 2458–2489.

Chirila, Andreea E. and Constantin, Ticu. 2016. "Mindset for Change, Motivational Persistence and Self-Efficacy in Personal Goal Achievement." *AI. I. Cuza University Psychology Series* 25, no. 1: 17–35.

Colwill, Deborah. 2015. "An Invitation to a Dialogue Table: Will You Come and Join Us?" *Christian Education Journal* 12, no. 1: 137–150.

Crenshaw, K. 1989. "Demarginalizing the Intersection of Race and Sex: A Black Feminist Critique of Antidiscrimination Doctrine, Deminist Theory and Antiracist Politics," *University of Chicago Legal Forum* 1: 139–167.

De Dreu, C.K., Nijstad, B.A., and van Knippenberg, D. 2008. "Motivated Information Processing in Group Judgment and Decision Making." *Personality and Social Psychology Review* 12: 22–49.

Dutta, Mohan J. 2011. *Communicating Social Change.* New York, NY: Routledge.

Edmonson, Amy. 1999. "Psychological Safety and Learning Behavior in Work Teams." *Administrative Science Quarterly* 44: 350–383.

Edmonson, Amy. 2004. "Psychological Safety, Trust and Learning: A Group Level Lens." In *Trust and Distrust in Organizations: Dilemmas and Approaches*, edited by R. Kramer and K. Cook, pp. 239–272. New York: Russell-Sage.

Edmonson, Amy. 2012. *Teaming.* San Francisco, CA: Jossey-Bass.

Edmonson, Amy, and Roloff, K.S. 2009. "Overcoming Barriers to Collaboration: Psychological Safety and Learning in Diverse Teams." In E. Salas, G.F. Goodwin, and C.S. Burke (Eds.) (pp. 183–208). New York, NY: Routledge/ Taylor and Francis Group.

Faust, Victoria, Christens, Brian D., Sparks, Shannon M.A., and Hilgendorf, Amy E. 2015. "Exploring Relationships among Organizational Capacity, Collaboration, and Network Change." *Psychosocial Intervention* 24: 125–131.

Fisher-Yoshida, Beth, Geller, Kathy Dee, and Schapiro, Steven A. 2009. *Innovations in Transformative Learning: Space, Culture and the Arts.* New York, NY: Peter Lang Publishing.

Freire, Paolo. 2000. *Pedagogy of the Oppressed.* New York, NY: Continuum.

Gasson, S., and Elrod, E.M. 2006. "Distributed Knowledge Coordination across Virtual Organization Boundaries." Proceedings of the 2006 International Conference on Information Systems. Milwaukee, Wisconsin: 947–966.

Giessner, Steffen R., van Knippenberg, Daan, van Ginkel, Wendy, and Sleebos, Ed. 2013. "Team Oriented Leadership: The Interactive Effects of Leader Group Prototypicality, Accountability and Team Identification." *Journal of Applied Psychology* 98, no. 4: 658–667.

Helland, M.R., and Winston, B.E. 2005. "Towards a Deeper Understanding of Hope and Leadership." *Journal of Leadership & Organizational Studies* 12: 42–55.

Howorth, Carole, Smith, Susan M., and Parkinson, Caroline. 2012. "Social Learning and Social Entrepreneurship Education." *Academy of Management Learning and Education* 11, no. 3: 371–389.

Isaacs, William. 1999. *Dialogue and the Art of Thinking Together*. New York, NY: Random House Inc.

Jaskyte, K. 2004. "Transformational Leadership, Organizational Culture, and Innovativeness in Nonprofit Organizations." *Nonprofit Management and Leadership* 15, no. 2: 153–168.

Jones, G.R. and J.M. George. 1998. "The Experience and Evolution of Trust: Implications for Cooperation and Teamwork." *Academy of Management Review* 23: 531–546.

Komives, Susan R., Wagner, Wendy, and Associates. 2017. *Leadership for a Better World*. San Francisco, CA: John Wiley & Sons.

Kotter, John. 2021. *Change*. Hoboken, NJ: Wiley.

Kouzes, J. and Posner, B. 2012. *The Leadership Challenge: How to Make Extraordinary Things Happen in Organizations* (5th ed.). San Francisco: CA: Jossey-Bass.

Kuenkel, Petra. 2016. *The Art of Leading Collectively: Co-Creating a Sustainable, Socially Just Future*. White River Junction, VT: Chelsea Green Publishing.

Levasseur, Robert E. 2013. "People Skills: Developing Soft Skills—A Change Management Perspective." *Interfaces* 43, no. 6: 566–571.

Levasseur, Robert E. 1991. "People skills: Self-awareness—a critical skill for MS/OR professionals." *Interfaces* 21, no. 1: 130–133.

Ling, Bin, Guo, Yue, and Chen, Dusheng. 2018. "Change Leadership and Employees' Commitment to Change." *Journal of Personnel Psychology* 17, no. 2: 83–93.

Liu, Xiao-Ping and Wang, Zhong-Ming. 2013. "Perceived Risk and Organizational Commitment: The Moderating Role of Organizational Trust." *Social Behavior and Personality* 41, no 2: 229–240.

Ospina, Sonia and Foldy, Erica. 2010. "Building Bridges from the Margins: The Work of Leadership in Social Change Organizations." *The Leadership Quarterly* 21: 292–307.

Owens, Bradley P. and Hekman, David R. 2012. "Modeling How to Grow: An Inductive Examination of Humble Leader Behaviors, Contingencies, and Outcomes." *Academy of Management Journal* 55, no. 4: 787–818.

Peters, Thomas J. and Waterman Jr, Robert H. 1982. "In Search of Excellence: Lessons from America's Best-Run Companies." *Administrative Science Quarterly* 28, no. 4: 621–624.

Plastrik, Peter, Taylor, Madeleine, and Cleveland, John. 2014. *Connecting to Change the World*. Washington, DC: Island Press.

Rogers, Everett M. 2003. *Diffusion of Innovations* (5th edition). New York, NY: Free Press.

Schein, Edgar. H. 2018. *Humble Leadership*. Oakland, CA: Berrett-Koehler Publishers, Inc.

Scott, Kim. 2017. *Radical Candor: Be A Kick-Ass Boss without Losing Your Humanity*. New York, NY: St. Martin's Press.

Seyranian, Viviane. 2014. "Social Identity Framing Communication Strategies for Mobilizing Social Change." *The Leadership Quarterly* 25: 468–486.

Shuman, Jeffrey and Twombly, Janice. 2010. "Collaborative Networks Are the Organization: An Innovation in Organizational Design and Management." *The Journal for Decision Makers* 35, no. 1: 1–13.

Stroh, David Peter. 2015. *Systems Thinking for Social Change*. White River Junction, VT: Chelsea Green Publishing.

Tetlock, P.E. 1992. "The Impact of Accountability on Judgment and Choice: Toward a Social Contingency Model." *Advances in Experimental Social Psychology* 25: 331–376.

Van der Voet, J., Kuipers, B.S., and Groeneveld, S. 2015. "Implementing Change in Public Organizations: The Relationship between Leadership and Affective Commitment to Change in a Public Sector Context." *Public Management Review* 18: 842–865.

Wanless, Shannon and Winters, Dana. 2018. "A Welcome Space for Taking Risks." *The Learning Professional* 39, no. 4: 41–44.

Westoby, Peter and Lyons, Kristen. 2017. "The Place of Social Learning and Social Movement in Transformative Learning: A Case Study of Sustainability Schools in Uganda." *Journal of Transformative Education* 15, no. 3: 223–240.

Worley, Christopher G., Willams, Thomas, and Lawlor III, Edward E. 2014. *The Agility Factor*. San Francisco, CA: Jossey-Bass.

Yankelovich, Daniel. 1999. *The Magic of Dialogue*. New York, NY: Touchstone.

Zulu, Itabari M. 2015. "TransAfrica as a Collective Enterprise: Exploring Leadership and Social Justice Attentiveness." *The Journal of Pan African Studies* 8, no. 9: 26–46.

Chapter 8

Practical Suggestions to Change the Way You Lead Change

Whenever I consult organizations on change, the number one request I receive is to clarify the "how." There's often a need to help others understand and take ownership over the action steps of moving from point A to point B. Simplifying the process is another way of setting others up for change success—it's people-centric. As the daughter of immigrants, I have frequently needed to translate the "how" for my parents; how to make purchases at the grocery store; how to open a bank account in the United States; or how to sign me up for the ballet classes I wanted to take. This ability to translate what we know to what we do is a learning experience that includes both proven strategy and informed experimentation. Translating change theory into practice can be a similar but necessary step to helping others take proven strategy and contextualize what works in their own contexts. Based on both the academic research and the data of the lived experiences of change leaders who participated in the research for this book, I have translated the top practical strategies that can help you change the way you lead change.

Implications of the Research

The relational communication strategies that non-profit social change agents use have implications for various organizations and stakeholders who are interested in any part of the spectrum of catalyzing change, connecting people toward change, and continuing momentum for change, or in learning how to lead a journey of change that honors and uplifts the people involved in the process. What follows are some suggestions for non-profit sector leaders, for-profit sector leaders, and leader developers.

Suggestions for Non-profit Sector Leaders

By nature of the organizational diversity of the non-profit sector itself, as well as the flatter systems and structures of organizational design,

DOI: 10.4324/9781003272243-9

non-profit sector leaders interact with layers of difference often unbound by hierarchical structures and subsequent regulations found in the for-profit sector. Further, building relationships for collective impact is critical in the non-profit sector, where both financial and people resources are continually needed. Therefore, relational communication strategies are very necessary for non-profit sector leaders seeking to increase their influence and impact. Non-profit leaders can take the following suggestions for more interconnected work:

Re-Learn by Asking Questions and Listening

Regardless of the length of one's tenure in the non-profit sector, asking questions and listening with the intent to genuinely learn from others can result in new insights or ideas, accountability to one's blind spots, and understanding of different dimensions of stakeholder needs. As change agents in this study suggested, shape rhythms of asking questions and listening as part of organizational practice to strengthen relationships and to consistently collect data that can inform future action. Change leaders also mentioned that timing for change happened at the pace of relational trust, often developed through curious listening. In our fast-paced, instant-gratification world, non-profit leaders can be counter-cultural by asking questions to learn and listening to discern new ways forward, thereby disrupting the norms of fragmentation to build or bolster interrelationships for collective impact.

Plan Touchpoints with Stakeholders

Intentionally plan communication touchpoints with stakeholders in order to imbed feedback loops into organizational systems that help non-profit leaders remain agile and adaptable to shifts in the change land-scape. According to the change leaders in this study, sometimes it is necessary to include assessable connections to stakeholders within job descriptions to keep one accountable to not losing sight of connecting with people on the ground. Touchpoints can include serving alongside others in one's context as well as planning fun activities with donors, braving speaking engagements, sending out newsletters, or attending off-site retreats with staff. Touchpoints give non-profit leaders access to stakeholder stories and perspectives, which feed back into the organization as possibilities for pivoting toward new directions. Touchpoints also diffuse information related to an organization's mission, thereby widening the possible reach of the desired change. Although time intensive, keeping stakeholders engaged via diverse communication touchpoints can be essential to change success.

Reconsider Hiring Tactics

Internal change agents exist in almost every community and have contextual expertise to contribute to a change process that is unparalleled to the knowledge of an external change agent. It is critical that non-profit leaders empower those they serve rather than creating dependency. As change leaders in this study remarked, non-profit leaders should want to work themselves out of a job. When possible, one significant way to continue momentum for a desired change is to hire from the community in which one serves. When an organization's employees begin to resemble the people who reside in the same community, deeper trust is developed as the organization becomes more imbedded within its context. Further, hires from the community can help keep the community's needs and hopes in the center of an organization's strategic plans, thereby keeping the organization accountable to the people it serves. By linking arms with community hires, non-profit leaders create internal channels for change diffusion by tapping into the roots of a community.

Engage Elephants in Dialogue

Non-profit leaders need to be courageous and have radical candor with stakeholders when necessary. Rather than avoiding elephant-in-the-room conversations, non-profit leaders can benefit from communicating truth in love for others. Leaders must be willing to engage offensive comments and divergent perspectives as well as convene dialogue to facilitate collective understanding and action. Keeping the principles of dialogue in mind, non-profit leaders are encouraged to normalize honest communication that is simultaneously respectful and dignifying. With complex social problems to solve, there is bound to be conflict and misunderstandings. Non-profit leaders need to initiate these hard conversations and facilitate relational bridging when necessary. Introduce language such as *generative conflict* or use metaphors such as the Kintsugi metaphor[1] to give people words and images of hope and innovation that can emerge from seemingly uncomfortable relational dynamics.

Suggestions for For-Profit Sector Leaders

Other sectors often look to the for-profit sector for leadership guidance and find valuable, transferable information. Likewise, for-profit leaders can gain wisdom from the non-profit change agents in this study, who provide critical insight for the increasing number of for-profit organizations that seek to be socially responsible, or to lead with a more people-centric approach. As corporate entities hire younger generations of people who desire meaningful work that contributes toward social impact, for-profit leaders can position themselves as well as their organizations for the changing workforce by taking the following suggestions:

Partner with Non-profit Leaders

In this increasingly interconnected world that demands greater socio-relational skills, for-profit leaders who partner with non-profit leaders can glean wisdom about relating to and communicating with people across differences. Specifically, as for-profit organizations design workplace structures and incentives to motivate employees' own desires to make the world a better place, for-profit leaders can invite and partner with non-profit leaders who are already doing the work of social change in their communities. Similar to the ways in which non-profit change agents come alongside internal change agents within the communities they serve, for-profit leaders can come alongside non-profit change agents to help accomplish the non-profit's own social change mission. This can be done by creating communication links between a for-profit and a non-profit so that information regarding societal shifts or needs can be shared. To inspire action that also simultaneously builds community, for-profits can create incentives for teams of employees to volunteer with non-profit partners who also need people to help serve and work on projects.

Moreover, for-profit leaders can convene roundtables or panel discussions where non-profit leaders are invited to educate and engage for-profit leaders in dialogue regarding social change. Further, for-profit organizations that have built-in foundations or corporate social responsibility branches can invite non-profit change agents as consultants to speak into process and systems design. With their unique relational lens, non-profit change agents can identify fragmentation and help build interconnections to influence a for-profit's social impact goals.

Follow the Example of Non-profit Leaders

It is highly likely that for-profit organizations have employees who act as internal change agents. Typically, the literature recognizes such people as social intrapreneurs (Mirvis 2017). Social intrapreneurs can look to the example of non-profit change agents and build an internal social network of trusting relationships that will act as a lever for change. Although social intrapreneurs carry unique knowledge and experience as an imbedded member of their organizations, they also have complex relationships by nature of their positionality within the hierarchy, especially in relation to those who have more power. These complex relationships mirror those in which non-profit change agents engage every day: relationships that require deep discernment, continual feedback through listening, consistent and honest conversations, and action that adds value to the lives of others. As such, social intrapreneurs can begin to build bridges of change within their organizations by acting as a facilitator of relationships who convenes people together, initiates conversations about uncomfortable topics, and expresses care and support for all parties involved.

Further, social intrapreneurs can disrupt the cultural norms of their organizations by introducing new information or ideas that can shift organizational culture. However, disruption can have a price within organizations that are used to a certain way of operating and can lead to internal resistance to change. By contrast, without disruption, social intrapreneurs may not become aware of possible shifts. By introducing new ideas or information and observing the reaction of others in the system, social intrapreneurs gain deeper insight into the kinds of change that may be worth advancing.

Suggestions for Leader Developers

Leader developers have direct access to and intimate contact with emerging change agents who desire to lead movements of social change. Leader developers include educators, professors, mentors, coaches, and student development professionals, to name a few. Non-profit change agents in this study shared their hope that young leaders would be better prepared to enter into non-profit work. With younger generations more interested in social impact than previous generations, it is recommended that leader developers consider the following suggestions:

Create Dialogical Learning Environments

Engaging young leaders in dialogue with one another can help them develop reflective capacity and self-awareness, both of which are important for non-profit social change work. Leader developers can cultivate spaces of multivocality where young leaders can come together to process their identities and their ideas, and confront one another's perspectives. This kind of social interaction can help model for young leaders the type of relational environment that can be challenging yet healthy. With non-profit social change work requiring constant engagement with diverse stakeholders, leader developers can serve young leaders well by giving dialogic opportunities to practice voicing one's own thoughts while also listening to the perspectives of others. In the classroom, a dialogue can be facilitated by the professor around a topic related to a lecture. In the world of higher education student development, staff can convene dialogue after experiential learning opportunities, or after special lectures given by guest speakers. With intentionality, dialogue can be strategically convened throughout a young leader's developmental journey.

Connect Classroom Teaching with Off-Campus Opportunities

Educators can work to integrate off-campus learning experiences with classroom teaching. Doing so provides young leaders opportunities to connect theory to practice and vice versa. Developing scholar practitioners can position young leaders to engage non-profit sector work with skills to use research, data, feedback, and on-the-ground experiences as an integrated practice of leading. This integration is necessary to lead social change, which we have discovered takes a constant posture of curiosity and learning. It is also critical that young leaders know how to receive and integrate information while staying true to their convictions and social change mission. Connecting classroom teaching with off-campus opportunities creates avenues to integrate mind, heart, and soul.

Teach Social Change Leadership

When coaching young people about leadership, a focus on non-profit social change leaders could add value to a young leader's toolkit. Placing leadership within the complexity of social change work can illumine the socio-emotional capacity that is demanded of leaders who want to serve others well and add value to society. One way to talk to young leaders about social change is to introduce Susan Komives' Social Change Model of Leadership Development (2017). Social change agents exhibit a combination of humility and courage that is needed in a world that is growing in diversity both in racial/ethnic representation and in people with different worldviews. Change agents may therefore interact with even more complexity and different layers of resistance in days to come. Developing relationships with others and communicating across differences may become even more critical in order to influence change that is wise and caring toward others.

Possibilities for Future Research

The present study was focused on the relational communication strategies of change agents in non-profit organizations and contributes to several streams of literature. Primarily, this study contributes to the non-profit sector literature, especially pertaining to non-profit social change institutions and non-profit change agents. Understanding the work of change agents in this field can bridge a gap in the literature on non-profit sector leadership by voicing the insights and concerns of change agent leaders who influence social change processes across diverse relational terrains. For example, this study helps fill a gap recognized in the literature, that "there is only minimal investigation into the different ways that exemplifies this social change role" of non-profit organizations (Shier and

Handy 2015, 2,583). Voicing the experiences of non-profit change agents illumines the highly relational work in which they engage, thereby providing guidance to other organizations as they adapt to an increasingly diverse workforce searching for meaningful, collaborative, and socially responsible work. Studying this segment of leaders also brings to the surface impactful practices and experiences from large, established non-profit social change institutions to provide learning transferability to leaders of small, new, or community-based non-profit organizations.

Additional research can be conducted, however, examining such topics as how non-profit social change institutions determine cross-sector partnerships, how resources are shared to accomplish collective social impact, and how non-profit organizations navigate unexpected relational challenges. Understanding the complexity that exists in these areas could provide clarity about very practical processes for non-profits that engage the daily reality of human unpredictability.

Second, this study also contributes to the literature on social entrepreneurship. Social entrepreneurs have an important role in addressing social problems (Stecker 2014). Therefore, it is not surprising that most non-profit change agents in this study self-identified as social entrepreneurs. The research on social entrepreneurship is still evolving with the continued need to understand how non-profit social entrepreneurs specifically develop the skills and knowledge to lead large-scale social change (Scheiber 2016). In their reflections on how they entered into the non-profit sector, as well as stories of their own paradigm shifts or learnings influenced through relationships, participants in this study revealed new relational dimensions of a social entrepreneur that go beyond personality traits or other dispositions. However, this study could be advanced by research that focuses on social entrepreneurs in primarily international contexts to discover parallels, if any, regarding the development of skills and knowledge as well as similarities and differences in relational communication strategies. Moreover, further research can be done to connect social entrepreneurship to research on social movements in order to learn more about social entrepreneurship's relationship to social causes rather than opportunities for exploitation. Last, more research can be done to further understand the social entrepreneur's portfolio of relationships and why collaborators may or may not change.

Third, this study contributes to the literature on social learning in non-profit organizations. Current literature states that the "greater the uncertainties organizations face, [the] greater the need for learning within organizations in all levels in order to cope with [a] diverse arena of uncertainty" (Ege, Esen, and Asik Disdar 2017, 441). Social change institutions face continual uncertainty with open systems that seek to adapt to shifts in the community around them. Therefore, participant comments about the importance of not only having a learning posture, but also continually learning through and acting on feedback from stakeholders, as well as their investment in helping others learn to change, reveal that non-profit change agents create a culture of learning within their organizations as a necessity to accomplishing their social change missions.

In addition, this study has illumined the centrality of multivocality in dialogue in the work of non-profit social change agents. Although not directly named in all parts of the change process, in their reflections of connecting relationships and communication together, the principles of dialogue (listening, respecting, suspending, and voicing) repeatedly surfaced. Dialogic practice gives people opportunities to learn about themselves and others via direct exposure and interaction with diverse individuals. The non-profit change agents in this study mentioned that they strategically convene dialogue to gather data in order to figure out how to better serve their constituents and connect people toward a desired change. In fact, the literature states, "dialogue ... has not been examined explicitly as the core mechanism by which strategic leaders influence the learning process at and between the individual, group and organizational levels" (Mazutis and Slawinski 2008, 438; Baker et al. 2005). As such, this study contributes to the literature by further connecting dialogue to the learning needed to advance change.

Despite this, further research can be done to study the influence of the timing of dialogue within a change process in building or impeding momentum for change. More generally speaking, it would also be interesting to explore in more depth the learning and development that happens in non-profit organizations. Questions such as "How do non-profits learn about and integrate best practices?" or "How does learning maintain the status quo?" or "How are young leaders prepared with collective capacities essential to non-profit social change work?" could be stand-alone research projects that stem from this study.

Conclusion

This book explored the relational communication strategies of 26 change agents in non-profit organizations. These change agents were known for their ability to discern the intimate interaction between the three dimensions of leading change well: people, process, and purpose, as described in previous chapters. The discerning change agent became the primary filter through which the realities, challenges, and hopes for change became known.

Listening to stories, asking questions, and seeking feedback were some means by which change agents discerned the current state of change within a context as well as the potential for future collective change agency. It was important to change leaders to do the work of discernment as a way to lead with humility and a posture of learning. It was also their way of keeping others before themselves with the desire to discern what could be most valuable to the people they served.

Change agents led change well when they genuinely loved people and sought to bring people together. Change agents worked diligently to develop trust with others and hesitated to move forward with change unless trust was built. In order to give themselves and their employees as much opportunity as possible to develop trusting relationships with others, change agents intentionally designed their organizations as open systems so that information could flow more freely across the walls of the organization. Further, when change agents discerned fragmentation or division between people, they did not hesitate to disrupt the status quo and to create opportunities for new ways of relating.

Change agents led change well when they communicated with respect and dignity with all stakeholders. By knowing their audience, change agents were able to have conversations with others that drew out information that would be helpful to achieve the change mission, or that inspired and motivated others to buy in to the change mission. Change agents convened dialogue as a way to cultivate the voices of others and center voices that are often in the margins of society. By centering the voices of others, change agents were better able to discern a new way forward through the different perspectives shared at the dialogue table. Change agents also co-constructed relational bridges with others through the communication of shared values and goals. These conversations created new partnerships for change and gave permission for others to communicate feedback regarding the authenticity of an organization's lived-out values.

Finally, change agents led change well when they continued momentum toward their social change mission by keeping the mission before themselves and others. Some of the ways they accomplished this were through consistent communication of the social change mission to various stakeholders, through developing new partnerships with other organizations aligned with the mission, and through stewarding their role in creating the most optimal conditions for learning that would enable others to draw closer to the change mission. Keeping the change mission as their North Star allowed change agents to innovate new ways of realizing the ultimate social change mission.

The hope for this book is that it illumines the tremendous good that non-profit change agents contribute to our world and how skilled they are at leading change. Through their sacrifice, hard work, wisdom, and courage, change agents who are good at what they do ultimately love people deeply. They are humble yet confident, courageous yet informed, and high-capacity people yet always learning. Always living in the grey areas of life, they prophetically move forward with hope for a new collective future.

Note

1 The Japanese art of putting broken pottery pieces back together with gold. https://www.bbc.co.uk/programmes/articles/326qTYw26156P9k92v8zr3C/ broken-a-pot-copy-the-japanese-and-fix- it-with-gold

References

Baker, A., Jensen, P., and Kolb, D. 2005. "Dialogue as Experiential Learning." *Management Learning* 36, no. 4: 411–427.

Ege, Tolga, Esen, Ayla, and Disdar, Asik. 2017. "Organizational Learning and Learning Organizations: An Integrative Framework." *The Journal of Management Economics and Business* 13, no. 2: 439–460.

Komives, Susan R., Wagner, Wendy, and Associates. 2017. *Leadership for a Better World*. San Francisco, CA: John Wiley & Sons.

Mazutis, Daina and Slawinski, Natalie. 2008. "Leading Organizational Learning through Authentic Dialogue." *Management Learning* 39, no. 4: 437–456.

Mirvis, Philip. 2017. "Redesigning Business to Serve Society: Joining Organization Development and Social Innovation." *OD Practitioner* 49, no. 3: 30–38.

Scheiber, Laura. 2016. "How Social Entrepreneurs in the Third Sector Learn from Life Experiences." *International Society for Third Sector Research* 27: 1694–1717.

Shier, M.L., and Handy, F. 2015. "From Advocacy to Social Innovation: A Typology of Social Change Efforts by Nonprofits." *International Society for Third-Sector Research* 26: 2581–2603.

Stecker, M.J. 2014. "Revolutionizing the Nonprofit Sector through Social Entrepreneurship." *Journal of Economic Issues* 48, no. 2: 349–357.

Chapter 9

Advice to Emerging Non-profit Change Agent Leaders

Whenever I'm sitting in the presence of a seasoned change leader, I never pass up an opportunity to be mentored in the moment. If anything has been underscored in this research is that change leaders consistently put on a learning posture to stay in tune with the times and the people before them. So, for anyone reading this book who is interested in growing into a better change leader, you're in luck! I've gleaned some great wisdom for you in this chapter. If time was available at the end of an interview, I asked the change leaders in my research study to reflect on advice she or he would want to give to the next generation of non-profit change agents. All who were asked were eager to share their thoughts and expressed deep excitement and care for young change agents interested in entering into non-profit social change work. This section summarizes some advice given by these seasoned change leaders as organized by the following five subthemes.

Subtheme 1: Have a "Posture of Humility and Learning"

One of the major subthemes that arose as advice to emerging leaders was the necessity of having a combined posture of humility and learning. Change leaders talked about the importance of humility and learning within the context of surrounding oneself with others who complement one's skills, admitting to not knowing and asking for help, learning from the very people one serves by listening to their needs, understanding oneself as well as one's work within the bigger perspective of change, embracing the "daily grind," and as one change leader said: "surrounding yourself with people who know more than you do—all the time" in order to learn from their wisdom. Another change leader also stated: "I think the first thing would be—listen carefully to the needs of your community and center them at the forefront." Similarly, another change leader expressed: "Talk less and listen more, ask more questions." Moreover, a change leader said: "I think the biggest thing is to just constantly be open to

DOI: 10.4324/9781003272243-10

constantly learning and evolving. And always be open to critique and constantly trying to find ways to do things better."

Having the desire to share a more sober perspective on changing the world with emerging leaders, one change leader expressed:

> When I was younger, I wanted to change the world. Now I just want to shine a light. Now that's still changing the world. I believe you get more of a humbler vision of who you are. You shine a light where you are and then it draws others to do that. And that's really how the world changes. It's not a big grandiose thing. Just be yourself. Just live courageously. Don't worry so much.

Another change leader also communicated that the work is not always glamorous, and therefore a posture of humility and learning is critical to ensure that leaders are present on the ground and in the day-to-day activities of an organization:

> I would say make sure that the ambition and the passion and the drive is coupled with a posture of humility and learning and putting in the early work. What I think can be very dangerous is the idea of assuming authority and leadership too quickly. I think there's significant value in showing up to work every single day doing something that may not be all that fun, all that exciting, or you know, you almost have to just kind of plug in and do the daily grind and be disciplined in that to actually learn some of what it takes to actually then step in and lead some things. Because honestly, for what we do, a lot of people might look at it and go, "Wow, that's so exciting and impactful, powerful," but there are so many things that we have to grind out on a daily basis that are very difficult, time consuming, emotionally burdensome; things that aren't "fun," but are absolutely necessary. And, some of the early work of grinding through things is very beneficial. So, I would definitely say a posture of learning is absolutely critical.

This same change leader continued to share that the "fake it till you make it" mentality is the opposite of a posture of humility and learning. He shared about an experience he had when seeking to expand his organization into India:

> And one other thing I want to add is that sometimes I hear people use the phrase—fake it until you make it. I think that is a terrible thing. I actually think that when I'm sitting across, for example, from a chartered accountant in India, which is like the equivalent of like a lawyer here in the US who would set up businesses, there is no way in the world I can fake understanding international tax law for

an Indian company that's going to be owned by a US non-profit. I think it would be ludicrous for me to fake as though I understand what you're saying. And so, I basically went into that meeting with a very clear conviction and with confidence that this is what we need to do, but I don't know Indian law, so teach me. And so, the whole idea of fake it until you make it—I don't think that's good advice. I think if you've got a very clear pathway laid out, conviction, and you're willing to work hard, then I think it's much better to say, "Listen, I'm not going away. This is not a flash in the pan. I'm committed to this thing. I'm relentless to make it happen, but I need your help and I need your expertise in this particular area because I'm not an expert here." And to try and fake it as though I am, that chartered accountant would see through me in the first five minutes. So, I think it's much better to take a posture of learning and humility with conviction and commitment than it is to fake it until you make it.

Subtheme 2: Keep "Eyes Wide Open"

Change leaders frequently mentioned the necessity of having the drive to clearly understand and become aware of the challenges of the non-profit sector, of the organization in which one desires to work, and of one's own conviction and calling to be a leader in the non-profit sector. Without the drive to discern these layers, participants warned emerging leaders of possible burnout, harming others by not understanding a problem's root causes, and experiencing a misfit between one's skills and work expectations, or between one's passions and organizational culture. For example, one change leader said: "Technically you need to understand the battlefield, the context. What are you even getting involved in?" Diving deeper into developing an understanding of the challenges, another change leader stated:

> Understand that the challenges we face are challenges for a reason; that if they were readily solvable or if there was a silver bullet, somebody would have found it already. There's typically going to be a pretty significant level of complexity. And so, enter with eyes wide open of whatever you believe the solution may be—it's probably not that. When you continue to peel back the onion on these issues, you find that there are significant levels of brokenness that are typically either systemic or societal issues that are just manifesting in these different symptoms. So, have the willingness to look at the root cause as well as the symptoms, which is really complicated and can feel defeating.

Another change leader talked about understanding challenges from her perspective as a female leader:

> My first thought is that it's a lot harder than it looks. For me, I'm the kind of person that's really driven by a challenge and I knew that I was getting into something big and it might fail and I was okay with that, but if it really worked then I'd be really proud of it. Like doing something is such a motivating factor for me, but I think too that there's a lot of things that aren't glamorous, right? There's a lot of frustrating moments for me as a woman. A lot of times where my peers have been much older males and I've been discounted, overlooked, left out of conversations countless times.

Other change leaders expressed that being aware of challenges internal to an organization is critical to being a leader. For example, a change leader talked about needing to test the assumptions of others when they challenged his ideas:

> I would always say test everything, test all the assumptions. A key driver for us would be that the women who are freed from the sex industry are going to be able to make our products. We had people early on telling us there is no way these women can make this stuff; they will not be able to do it. There's no way. So, we had to challenge that and test the assumption. So, there's this constant need to be aware of what we're assuming and then testing it to prove it. I think it's really key and then being able to recognize when we are wrong. We need to pivot here to be able to move forward without compromising the overall mission and the values of the organization.

Along the same lines, another change leader shared specifically about discerning one's fit with a respective organization by seeking awareness of possible internal challenges:

> Make sure that you are very aligned and really passionate about the mission of the organization. But, it's also very important for you to have a cultural fit as well. I've seen circumstances where you may be passionate about the mission, but every organization has its unique culture and you really need to figure out if you would do well in that culture because that goes a long way.

Finally, Christian participants in particular underscored the significance of taking the time to discern one's calling into non-profit leadership. One change leader passionately declared:

People want to lead everything. They want to create their own non-profit. We need leaders, but we need people who are called. And if people are called into other roles, we need more people who will really embrace that and see that as equally valuable. If you're not called to lead, I think it's awful and it's definitely not fun because it's definitely not what people think it is from the outside. So, think twice. Leading is not always fun. It's overrated. Highly, highly overrated.

Likewise, another Christian change leader stated:

A big lesson that I've learned is to be open to where the Lord leads you and what you may do and it may be for a season and it may be for a long time—to really hold things loosely. I think the danger of being so passionate about something is that you can really make it your own and your whole identity is wrapped up in that. Then, if God takes that away from you, that'll be really painful and hurtful. And so, I learned to hold things very loosely; that at any moment God could tap me and say, "Now I want you to serve over here." To be very open to that.

Yet another Christian change leader affirmed the stories above:

My advice is to pray and really make sure that they know that this is what God's calling them to do. And my advice to a lot of young leaders who feel like God's calling them to do something is wait until it's so painful that you can't not do it and you have to do it. If God truly is calling you to do something and there's no question about that, then God will equip you with everything you need. In other words, if God's called you to do something, it's already finished. This is hard work and it would be really disastrous work if you weren't really in the center of God's will and if God didn't provide and protect and lead and guide and do all those things—all those things that only God can do. So, my advice is not only to spend some time praying about it, but really wrestle with God over it. And don't do it until you're clear that you have to do it or you'll die. And if that's what God wants them to do, God will make it painfully clear. The hardest thing to do is pray and wait on God. But, it's the smartest thing to do. Don't do it unless you feel called to do it. And even when you feel God's calling, test that and make sure.

Subtheme 3: Embrace Change

Several change leaders shared their hopes that emerging leaders would not only believe change is possible, but also be open to change and, in fact, embrace it. Undergirding their advice was their desire to encourage emerging change agents in their change-making potential. One change leader proclaimed enthusiastically: "I would say that you absolutely can change the world. It is possible." Another change leader mentioned that if his team had not developed "an attitude of openness to change," his organization would not have grown to what it is currently:

> I think I would quickly say to develop an attitude of openness to change. Change will happen regardless of what you do. It will be what it's going to be. And so, you really need to be ready and able to try new things. Our motto here is always—let's try a little bit of it and see how it works and we can shed it off if it doesn't work too well and we'll go big with it if it does. You must be able to start small on things, not knowing how they're going to work out for sure. Some of the things we thought were dead ringers, you know, this is really going to be good—two years later, we shed it because it didn't work the way we thought it was going to. Now, we could have let our ego stay in the way—"This is OUR program, this is the way WE do it." But you can't really do that and be successful. You have to be flexible enough to be able to change as you go; accept change in your mind. Just be ready for that constant change, be open it. Not only be ready for it, be ready to embrace it. I would say if I were going to give advice to anybody, it would be that.

One change leader who identified as a Christian Asian–American participant expressed her hope that emerging leaders would remember to recognize and embrace different methods of change-making:

> So much about communication is oral and about speaking and I think there's so much communication that happens that isn't spoken. So, I think a lot of White men do all their communication and their leading through speaking and talking and it's sort of noisy. But I also think there are a lot of Asian women who also drop the mic—I have a public speaking portion of my work as a significant portion of my work—but I think also wanting to cultivate the importance of the ability to create spaces for other voices is a significant part of communication and coalition building and change-making. The deep ability to elevate and prop up others; so not just building platforms, but building true and authentic partnerships.

Subtheme 4: Grow in Self-Awareness

Another piece of advice that change leaders frequently shared was their charge to emerging leaders to grow in their self-awareness. This charge was rooted in a genuine care to communicate that the impact of a leader's work is significantly influenced by who the leader is. Therefore, the more self-aware leaders are, the more likely their impact will be grounded in reality rather than disillusionment. For example, one change leader expressed that an unclear understanding of one's own values and passions can create barriers to achieving one's mission:

> Create your own core values and be consistent with them. I would also say to really get clear with the kind of work you really want to do. What is it that you really believe in? What do you really care about at the end of the day? Because if you say you want to help people grow or change and that's what the organization is created to do, or was on paper created to do, but you've set your own limit internally, then you're just hurting people. At the end of the day, your organization is not serving in the way that you intended it to serve. It starts with yourself first and then into an organization.

Speaking more specifically about the possible distractions that leaders can face, another change leader mentioned the importance of being secure in one's identity and aware of motivational influencers:

> There are days when I look back on my career, and a lot of times I did things without even knowing it—sometimes because I was trying to prove myself to other people around me. That became my driving factor. So, I think now I'm a little bit more content with who I am because I feel like I don't have as much to prove. I don't know if it's just a different stage in my life. I also think it's hard to tell young people that because I think during those younger years you're trying to find out who you are. My advice is to keep your identity in God and to believe that God will open the right steps for you. I think when we try to pursue our own individuality and our own personal accomplishments, it distracts us from where we're supposed to be.

Another change leader also talked about the potential of identity confusion without self-awareness:

> I think this spans beyond a non-profit leadership role, but when as an entrepreneur you're starting something new, it becomes really hard to separate that out of my own personal identity. And if I had a bad day at work, if I lost a funding opportunity or took a hit in any way, that that didn't mean my life was over. And I had to separate those things out and create a healthy support system outside of my work life in ways that weren't inundated day in and day out with that. Left to my own devices I will live and breathe and die

everything because I built it. And so, it's important to understand what's necessary and what's healthy and how to have boundaries around all of those processes.

Another change leader placed the need for self-awareness within the context of her own work freeing victims of sexual violence:

> This is something my spiritual director reminds me of very often—you can't heal the world unless you yourself are first healed. And so, I would say that is the most important thing is to work on your own healing, and advocacy for yourself, and your own journey of transformation, and your own whatever it is, work on that. Work on that together as you work on the issues of the world. It's not separate. It's actually together. I always say that the violence we see in the world is all a result of the violence within ourselves. I don't believe that people are born as rapists or as inherently violent people. But, because it's not worked on internally, that's how it manifests so violently in the world. And so, to do that internal work of healing your own violence against yourself, whether it be the words that you say to yourself, the things that you think about yourself—heal those wounds first so that your violence does not spread into the community, whether knowingly or unknowingly.

Another change leader also shared how growing in awareness of her hurried life helped her become a better leader. As a result of this insight, she wanted to tell emerging leaders:

> My husband and I called a mentor of ours when we were about to make a job change and asked for advice. And honestly, at the time when he said what he said, we both thought, "Man, we were expecting something way more profound." But, he said, "You must ruthlessly eliminate hurry." Overall, there's a difference between being busy and being hurried and how do I ruthlessly eliminate hurry? And I just struggle with that. I still do. But, on the second or the minutes in a day when I can get there, it is so good. And it feels like all of that space—that's the right place to stand. Yeah, that's what I would say.

One change leader expressed that taking advantage of challenging times to grow a deeper awareness of self was key to effective leadership:

> The first thing that comes to mind is to pay attention to the foundations and look for the opportunities to go deep. Often what happens is when you're in a situation with ever-increasing

leadership, there are ebbs and flows of quiet times or times of isolation or alienation or wilderness times. And every time you catch one of those, go deep on something. I think people have a tendency to spin their wheels during those times because there's not much that's being asked of you during those times. But, take every opportunity to go deep. Because what happens is when you are in spaces of ever-increasing leadership, it is twice or three times as hard to get the depth that you need and so you find yourself really drawing on the deep roots that were developed in the well-watering that happened over many seasons. So, I think there's something about personal character, personal integrity, and a personal faithfulness when you have nothing or a very small scope—make sure that you build those things in deep because I've just seen too many people get top heavy and it just crushes them due to the lack of foundation. So, it's the ability to go to scripture, even simple things like exercising or knowing how to be able to dial down at night and sleep.

Subtheme 5: Be Your Best Advocate

Finally, some female participants wanted to remind emerging leaders to be their own best advocate by remaining courageous and voicing opinions when necessary. Giving advice to her younger self, one change leader said:

> If I were talking to myself, I would say don't be afraid of your voice. Don't be scared to speak up for what you know to be right even if that means you might sound a little silly. You are your own best advocate, so advocate for yourself more. I think my natural disposition is not to be boastful, but I think I, for a long time, was not boastful to a fault, to the point where I would attribute credit to other people or to the team. It took me a while to realize that you can definitely support the team, but also talk about the piece that you played and that you are important. You are an important part of the team. To claim that you are an important part of a team is not a bad thing. It's not boastful, it's not prideful, it's not whatever other negative BS the world tries to drill into you, specifically as a woman and a person of color. Sometimes people won't see you if you don't say it. So, advocate for yourself. You kick ass and people need to know that.

Sharing a similar story, but within the context of fundraising, another change leader voiced:

One thing I wish I would've known earlier and I think I would tell people early on is basically, don't be apologetic for what you're doing. One of the things in non-profit work is you often have to ask people for money, and you have to make them care about something. You have to tell them you need their dollars because it's going to get this thing for this person, but you're not getting a laptop when you give me these dollars. So, I think sometimes you can feel really apologetic about it, or like you don't want to ask them for money. Don't be apologetic about it, and don't feel like you have to bend your message to fit the person. So, I'd say don't be apologetic and be a leader in the conversation because that's where that work is gonna happen. Sometimes it's not going to work out and that's fine because people are going to fund what they want to fund and you still have to be who you are despite all those things.

Closing Thoughts

I stand on the shoulders of many change agents who have gone before me. My entrepreneurial grandfather who forever redefined who can work and contribute to South Korea's economic engine; my parents who immigrated to the United States and changed the trajectory of our lives for the better in a foreign country; many mentors who helped me find my true voice and step into the change leader I always knew I was; and each change leader who agreed to participate in this research because they thought it important to share their experiences, not for the sake of platform, but rather, to elevate the valuable work of their communities, their people, and the non-profit sector they've committed their lives to. My hope is that this book and the very people on its pages are some of those shoulders for you too.

Index

vision
  big-perspective 134
  clear 94, 96
  collective 70
  humbler 150
  initial 21
  new 81
  shared 73
vocational choices 19
voices
  centering 67, 123
  diverse 38, 86, 123
  marginal 5, 45
  marginalized 46, 88
  new 85, 123
volunteering 21–22
volunteers 76, 93, 113–14, 142
vulnerability 65

wisdom 13, 18, 51, 72, 103–4, 112, 122, 127, 141, 147, 149

learned 81
women 20, 24–27, 79, 152
  young 27
work environment 111
workforce searching, diverse 12, 145
workshops 87
world
  changing 3, 29
  corporate 40
  equitable 18
  ideal 100
  instant-gratification 140
  post-bureaucratic 30
  post-industrial 30
worldviews 46, 144

younger generations 141, 143
young leaders in dialogue 143
youth, marginalized urban 23

zones, uncomfortable 78